Highlights

KNOCK KNOCK!

The Biggest, Best Joke Book EVER

Highlights Press
Honesdale, Pennsylvania

Contributing Illustrators: David Coulson, Kelly Kennedy,
Pat N. Lewis, Neil Numberman, Rich Powell, Kevin Rechin,
Rick Stromoski, Pete Whitehead

Published by Highlights Press
815 Church Street
Honesdale, Pennsylvania 18431
ISBN: 978-1-62979-889-9
Manufactured in Robbinsville, NJ, USA
Mfg. 10/2020

First edition
Visit our website at Highlights.com.
10 9 8 7 6 5

Contents

Animal Antics . . . . 8 . . . .

Silly Sports . . . . 34 . . .

Funny Food . . . . 46 . . . .

Girl Giggles: A–L . . . . 70 . . . .

Cat and Dog Crackups . . . . 96 . . . .

Musical Mirth . . . . 106 . . . .

Famous and Funny . . . . 114 . . . .

Boy Belly Laughs: A–L . . . . 124 . . . . .

Sugar-Coated Laughs . . . . 146 . . . .

Household Humor 156

Holiday Ha-Has . . . . 178 . . . .

Girl Giggles: M-Z . . . . 188 . . . .

Big Bug Laughs . . . . 206 . . . .

School Sillies . . . . 214 . . . .

Boy Belly Laughs: M-Z 226

Family Funnies . . . . 242 . . . .

Get the Door Already! . . . . 248 . . . .

Laugh Around the World . . . . 270 . .

Wacky Weather . . . . 294 . . . .

This and That . . . . 302 . .

Last Laughs . . . . 326 . . . . . .

Animal Antics

Knock, knock.
Who's there?
Gorilla.
Gorilla who?
Gorilla me a burger, please. I'm hungry.

Knock, knock.
Who's there?
Athena.
Athena who?
Athena mouse run past your door!

Knock, knock.
Who's there?
Whale.
Whale who?
Whale, whale, whale. I see your door is locked again.

Knock, knock.
Who's there?
Toad.
Toad who?
Toad you I knew a good knock-knock joke.

Knock, knock.
Who's there?
Goat.
Goat who?
Goat to the door and find out!

Knock, knock.
Who's there?
Gibbon.
Gibbon who?
Gibbon the circumstances, I'd
rather stay home.

Knock, knock.
Who's there?
Gecko.
Gecko who?
Gecko-ing or you'll be late for school!

Knock, knock.
Who's there?
Beaver E.
Beaver E. who?
Beaver E. quiet and nobody will hear us.

Knock, knock.
Who's there?
Gopher.
Gopher who?
Gopher help. I'm stuck in the mud!

Knock, knock.
Who's there?
Aardvark.
Aardvark who?
Aardvark a hundred miles for you.

Knock, knock.
Who's there?
Knock.
Knock who?
Knock-a-doodle-doo!

Knock, knock.
Who's there?
Giraffe.
Giraffe who?
Giraffe anything to eat? I'm hungry!

Knock, knock.
Who's there?
Tuna.
Tuna who?
Tuna your radio down—I can't get to sleep!

Knock, knock.
Who's there?
Toucan.
Toucan who?
Toucan play this game.

Knock, knock.
Who's there?
Hippo.
Hippo who?
Hippo birthday to you!

Knock, knock.
Who's there?
Owl.
Owl who?
Owl aboard!

Knock, knock.
Who's there?
A herd.
A herd who?
A herd you were home, so I came over.

Knock, knock.
Who's there?
Claws.
Claws who?
Claws the window—it's cold in here!

Knock, knock.
Who's there?
Alberts.
Alberts who?
Do Alberts fly south for the winter?

Knock, knock.

Who's there?

Aurora.

Aurora who?

Aurora just came from that polar bear.

Knock, knock.

Who's there?

Alli.

Alli who?

Alligator, that's who.

Knock, knock.

Who's there?

Hens.

Hens who?

Hens up, we've got you surrounded!

Knock, knock.

Who's there?

Moo.

Moo who?

Make up your mind! Are you a cow or an owl?

Knock, knock.
Who's there?
Cows go.
Cows go who?
No, cows go moo!

Knock, knock.
Who's there?
Interrupting cow.
Interrup—
MOOOOO!

Knock, knock.
Who's there?
Dragon.
Dragon who?
These jokes are dragon on and on.

Knock, knock.
Who's there?
T. rex.
T. rex who?
There's a T. rex at your
door and you want to
know its name?!

Knock, knock.
Who's there?
Sparrow.
Sparrow who?
Sparrow me the details and let me in.

Knock, knock.
Who's there?
Lionel.
Lionel who?
Lionel bite you if you put your head in its mouth.

Knock, knock.
Who's there?
Ocelot.
Ocelot who?
You ocelot of questions, don't you?

Knock, knock.
Who's there?
Ostrich.
Ostrich who?
Ostrich my arms up to the sky.

Knock, knock.
Who's there?
Shellfish.
Shellfish who?
Don't be shellfish, open up and share!

Knock, knock.
Who's there?
Hyena.
Hyena who?
Hyena tree sits the beautiful bald eagle.

Knock, knock.
Who's there?
Weasel.
Weasel who?
Weasel while you work.

Knock, knock.
Who's there?
Chicken.
Chicken who?
Better chicken the oven—something's burning.

Knock, knock.
Who's there?
Halibut.
Halibut who?
Halibut we go to the movies tonight?

Knock, knock.

Who's there?
Alpaca.
Alpaca who?
Alpaca the trunk, you pack-a the suitcase.

Knock, knock.
Who's there?
Baby owl.
Baby owl who?
Baby owl see you later or baby owl just call you.

Knock, knock.
Who's there?
Icy.
Icy who?
Icy a big polar bear.

Knock, knock.
Who's there?
Heifer.
Heifer who?
Heifer dollar is better than none.

Knock, knock.
Who's there?
Bison.
Bison who?
Bison new shoes. Those are worn out!

Knock, knock.
Who's there?
Woodchuck.
Woodchuck who?
Woodchuck come to our party if we
invited him?

Knock, knock.
Who's there?
Bat.
Bat who?
Bat you can't guess.

Knock, knock.
Who's there?
Ibis.
Ibis who?
Ibis just leaving.

Knock, knock.
Who's there?
Iguana.
Iguana who?
Iguana hold your hand.

Knock, knock.
Who's there?
Kanga.
Kanga who?
Kangaroo, silly!

Knock, knock.
Who's there?
Who.
Who who?
I didn't know you spoke Owl!

Knock, knock.

Who's there?

Possum.

Possum who?

Possum food, please. I'm hungry!

Knock, knock.
Who's there?
Viper.
Viper who?
Viper runny nose, please.

Knock, knock.
Who's there?
Stork.
Stork who?
Better stork up on food before the storm.

Knock, knock.
Who's there?
Monkey.
Monkey who?
Monkey won't fit. That's why I knocked!

Knock, knock.
Who's there?
Deduct.
Deduct who?
Deduct went "Quack, quack."

Knock, Knock.
Who's there?
Dinosaur.
Dinosaur who?
Dinosaurs don't go "who." They go "ROAR!"

Knock, knock.
Who's there?
Quack.
Quack who?
You quack me up with all these knock-knock jokes.

Knock, knock.

Who's there?

Moose.

Moose who?

Moose you be so nosy?

Knock, knock.
Who's there?
Otter.
Otter who?
You otter open the door and let me in.

Knock, knock.
Who's there?
Cock-a-doodle.
Cock-a-doodle who?
Not cock-a-doodle who, you silly chicken,
cock-a-doodle-doo!

Knock, knock.
Who's there?
Cod.
Cod who?
Cod you red-handed with all my gummy worms!

Knock, knock.
Who's there?
Llama.
Llama who?
"Llama Yankee Doodle Dandy . . ."

Knock, knock.
Who's there?
Manatee.
Manatee who?
Manatee you made needs more lemon and sugar.

Knock, knock.
Who's there?
Mice.
Mice who?
Mice to meet you.

Knock, knock.
Who's there?
Wren.
Wren who?
Wren you're finished, please put it away.

Knock, knock.
Who's there?
Urchin.
Urchin who?
Urchin has a dimple.

Knock, knock.
Who's there?
Udder.
Udder who?
Would you like to hear an-udder knock-knock joke?

Knock, knock.
Who's there?
Grrr.
Grrr who?
Are you a bear or an owl?

Knock, knock.
Who's there?
Odor.
Odor who?
Odor skunks are wiser than younger skunks.

Knock, knock.
Who's there?
Rhino.
Rhino who?
Rhino every knock-
knock joke there is.

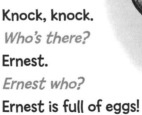

Knock, knock.
Who's there?
Ernest.
Ernest who?
Ernest is full of eggs!

Knock, knock.
Who's there?
Cowhide.
Cowhide who?
Cowhide if she sees you coming.

Knock, knock.
Who's there?
Mammoth.
Mammoth who?
Mammoth is sthuck 'cause I'th
been eatin' peanut buther.

Knock, knock.
Who's there?
Why do owls go.
Why do owls go who?
Because that's how they talk, silly!

Knock, knock.
Who's there?
Panther.
Panther who?
Panther what I wear on my legth.

Knock, knock.
Who's there?
Michelle.
Michelle who?
Michelle has a hermit crab inside.

Knock, knock.
Who's there?
Rabbit.
Rabbit who?
Rabbit carefully—it's a present for my mom.

Knock, knock.
Who's there?
Pig.
Pig who?
Pig up your feet or you'll trip.

Knock, knock.
Who's there?
Wallaby.
Wallaby who?
Wallaby a monkey's uncle!

Knock, knock.
Who's there?
Rattle.
Rattle who?
Rattle eat that cheese if we forget to put it away.

Knock, knock.
Who's there?
Ox.
Ox who?
Ox me nice and I'll take you out for ice cream.

Knock, knock.

Who's there?

Cow.

Cow who?

Cow much longer are you going to put
up with all this knocking?

Knock, knock.

Who's there?

Owls.

Owls who?

Of course they do—everybody knows that.

Knock, knock.

Who's there?

Robin.

Robin who?

Robin banks is wrong.

Silly Sports

Knock, knock.

Who's there?

Avery.

Avery who?

Avery time I swing at a bad pitch, I strike out.

Knock, knock.
Who's there?
Lucinda.
Lucinda who?
Lucinda strap on my bike helmet—it's too tight!

Knock, knock.
Who's there?
Randy.
Randy who?
Randy mile in eight minutes.

Knock, knock.
Who's there?
Jethro.
Jethro who?
Jethro the boat and stop asking questions.

Knock, knock.
Who's there?
Ratio.
Ratio who?
Ratio to the end of the street!

Knock, knock.
Who's there?
Bjorn.
Bjorn who?
Bjorn to run.

Knock, knock.
Who's there?
Rush hour.
Rush hour who?
Rush hour quarterback and we'll block you.

Knock, knock.
Who's there?
Alice.
Alice who?
Alice our best punter.

Knock, knock.
Who's there?
Alana.
Alana who?
Alana on my head after I tripped
over your skateboard.

Knock, knock.
Who's there?
Andy.
Andy who?
Andy shoots, Andy scores!

Knock, knock.
Who's there?
Dissenter.
Dissenter who?
Dissenter fielder catches a lot of fly balls.

Knock, knock.
Who's there?
Battle.
Battle who?
Battle hit that ball right out of the park!

Knock, knock.
Who's there?
Bobbin.
Bobbin who?
Bobbin the pool, but he can't swim.

Knock, knock.
Who's there?
Anya.
Anya who?
Anya mark, get set, go!

Knock, knock.
Who's there?
Canoe.
Canoe who?
Canoe come out and play with me?

Knock, knock.
Who's there?
Omega.
Omega who?
Omega best player win.

Knock, knock.
Who's there?
Myron.
Myron who?
Myron around the track made me tired.

Knock, knock.
Who's there?
Chick.
Chick who?
Chick out my new skateboard!

Knock, knock.
Who's there?
Tennis.
Tennis who?
Tennis five plus five.

Knock, knock.
Who's there?
Philip.
Philip who?
Philip your pool. I want to go swimming!

Knock, knock.
Who's there?
Meow.
Meow who?
Take meow to the
ball game!

Knock, knock.
Who's there?
Dennis.
Dennis who?
Dennis is my favorite sport.

Knock, knock.
Who's there?
Hoyt.
Hoyt who?
Hoyt myself riding my bike.

Knock, knock.
Who's there?
Gwen.
Gwen who?
Gwen fishin'.

Knock, knock.
Who's there?
Uriah.
Uriah who?
Keep Uriah on the ball!

Knock, knock.
Who's there?
Tess.
Tess who?
Tess me the softball.

Knock, knock.
Who's there?
Tee.
Tee who?
Tee if you can guess who this is.

Knock, knock.

Who's there?

Polo.

Polo who?

Polo-ver, you're under arrest.

Funny Food

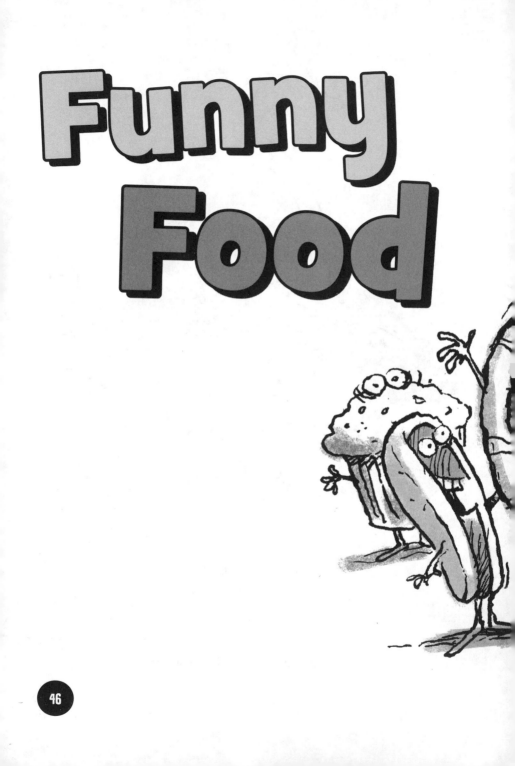

Knock, knock.

Who's there?

Pizza.

Pizza who?

Pizza really nice guy.

Knock, knock.
Who's there?
Ada.
Ada who?
Ada lot for lunch, so now I'm really full.

Knock, knock.
Who's there?
Bacon.
Bacon who?
Bacon a chocolate cake for your birthday.

Knock, knock.
Who's there?
Almond.
Almond who?
Almond the other side of the door.

Knock, knock.
Who's there?
Muffin.
Muffin who?
There's muffin the matter with me—
I'm doing fine!

Knock, knock.
Who's there?
Pickle.
Pickle who?
Pickle little flower to give to your mother.

Knock, knock.
Who's there?
Mushroom.
Mushroom who?
There's mushroom for improvement on that last joke.

49

Knock, knock.
Who's there?
Beets.
Beets who?
Beets me.

Knock, knock.
Who's there?
Cereal.
Cereal who?
Cereal pleasure to meet you!

Knock, knock.
Who's there?
Pecan.
Pecan who?
Pecan somebody
your own size.

Knock, knock.
Who's there?
Pastor.
Pastor who?
Pastor potatoes. I'm hungry!

Knock, knock.
Who's there?
Bean.
Bean who?
Bean fishing lately?

Knock, knock.
Who's there?
X.
X who?
X for breakfast—scrambled, please!

Knock, knock.
Who's there?
Wendy Waiter.
Wendy Waiter who?
Wendy Waiter gets here, order me a cheeseburger.

Knock, knock.
Who's there?
Frankfurter.
Frankfurter who?
Frankfurter lovely present.

Knock, knock.
Who's there?
Barbie.
Barbie who?
Barbie Q.

Knock, knock.

Who's there?

Veal chop.

Veal chop who?

Veal chop around and find some bargains.

Knock, knock.

Who's there?

Stew.

Stew who?

Stew early to go to bed.

Knock, knock.

Who's there?

Alec.

Alec who?

Alec tea, but I don't like coffee.

Knock, knock.

Who's there?

Goblin.

Goblin who?

Goblin your food will give you a tummyache.

Knock, knock.
Who's there?
Dimitri.
Dimitri who?
Dimitri is where de hamburgers grow.

Knock, knock.
Who's there?
Celery.
Celery who?
Celery dance?

Knock, knock.
Who's there?
Cheese.
Cheese who?
Cheese a very smart girl.

Knock, knock.
Who's there?
Peas.
Peas who?
Peas, can you come out and play?

Knock, knock.
Who's there?
Omelet.
Omelet who?
Omelet smarter than you think.

Knock, knock.

Who's there?
Banana.
Banana who?
Knock, knock.
Who's there?
Banana.
Banana who?
Knock, knock.
Who's there?
Orange.
Orange who?
Orange you glad
I didn't say banana?

55

Knock, knock.

Who's there?

Cantaloupe.

Cantaloupe who?

Cantaloupe tonight—I forgot the wedding ring.

Knock, knock.

Who's there?

Carrot.

Carrot who?

Don't you carrot all about me?

Knock, knock.
Who's there?
Armor.
Armor who?
Armor snacks coming? I'm starving.

Knock, knock.
Who's there?
Curry.
Curry who?
Curry the groceries in, please.

Knock, knock.
Who's there?
Irish stew.
Irish stew who?
Irish stew in the name of the law.

Knock, knock.
Who's there?
Hummus.
Hummus who?
Let me in and I'll hummus a tune.

Knock, knock.
Who's there?
Ida.
Ida who?
Ida sandwich for lunch today. Do you want one?

Knock, knock.
Who's there?
Apple.
Apple who?
Apple on the door, but it won't open!

Knock, knock.
Who's there?
Hammond.
Hammond who?
Hammond eggs with toast is delicious!

Knock, knock.
Who's there?
Guava.
Guava who?
Guava good time.

Knock, knock.
Who's there?
Pumpkin.
Pumpkin who?
A pumpkin fill up your flat tire.

Knock, knock.
Who's there?
Cash.
Cash who?
No thanks, but I'd love some peanuts.

Knock, knock.
Who's there?
Jupiter.
Jupiter who?
Jupiter fly in my soup?

Knock, knock.
Who's there?
Lettuce.
Lettuce who?
Lettuce in, please!

Knock, knock.
Who's there?
Raisin.
Raisin who?
We're raisin our hands before we speak.

Knock, knock.
Who's there?
Pesto.
Pesto who?
I hate to make a pesto myself, but I'm going to keep knocking until you open.

Knock, knock.
Who's there?
Avocado.
Avocado who?
Avocado an awful cold. *Ah-choo!*

Knock, knock.

Who's there?

Cook.

Cook who?

Hey, who are you
calling a cuckoo?

Knock, knock.
Who's there?
Crispin.
Crispin who?
Crispin and crunchy is how I like my cereal.

Knock, knock.
Who's there?
Kiwi.
Kiwi who?
Kiwi go to the store?

Knock, knock.
Who's there?
Cumin.
Cumin who?
Cumin side—it's freezing out there.

Knock, knock.
Who's there?
Honeycomb.
Honeycomb who?
Honeycomb your hair—
it's tangled.

Knock, knock.
Who's there?
Figs.
Figs who?
Figs me a sandwich, please.

Knock, knock.
Who's there?
Honeydew.
Honeydew who?
Honeydew you love me?

Knock, knock.
Who's there?
Falafel.
Falafel who?
I falafel my bike and hurt my knee.

Knock, knock.
Who's there?
Dairy.
Dairy who?
Dairy goes! Let's catch him!

Knock, knock.
Who's there?
Distressing.
Distressing who?
Distressing has too
much vinegar.

Knock, knock.
Who's there?
Emile.
Emile who?
Emile fit for a king.

Knock, knock.
Who's there?
Veal.
Veal who?
Veal always love you.

Knock, knock.
Who's there?
Goudas.
Goudas who?
She's as goudas can be.

Knock, knock.
Who's there?
Fajita.
Fajita who?
Fajita another thing,
I'll be stuffed.

Knock, knock.
Who's there?
Ketchup.
Ketchup who?
Ketchup with me and
you'll find out!

Knock, knock.
Who's there?
Don.
Don who?
Don talk with your mouth full.

Knock, knock.
Who's there?
Ham.
Ham who?
Ham I getting warmer?

Knock, knock.
Who's there?
Four eggs.
Four eggs who?
Four eggs-ample, a tomato is actually a fruit.

Knock, knock.
Who's there?
Mac.
Mac who?
Mac and cheese.

Knock, knock.
Who's there?
Toast.
Toast who?
Toast were the days.

Knock, knock.
Who's there?
Punch.
Punch who?
Not me, please!

Wheeee!

Knock, knock.
Who's there?
Quiche.
Quiche who?
Can I have a hug and a quiche?

Knock, knock.
Who's there?
Olive.
Olive who?
Olive the pizza was gone before I got a slice!

Knock, knock.
Who's there?
Pete.
Pete who?
Pete-za delivery!

Knock, knock.
Who's there?
Ricotta.
Ricotta who?
Ricotta new bike. Want to see him ride?

Knock, knock.
Who's there?
Phyllis.
Phyllis who?
Phyllis cup up with water, please.
I'm thirsty!

Knock, knock.
Who's there?
Sweden.
Sweden who?
Sweden sour chicken is my favorite.

Knock, knock.
Who's there?
Sheik.
Sheik who?
Sheik the juice carton before you pour.

Knock, knock.
Who's there?
Pasta.
Pasta who?
Pasta salt and pepper, please.

Knock, knock.
Who's there?
Nacho cheese.
Nacho cheese who?
That is nacho cheese,
so give it back!

Knock, knock.

Who's there?

Waffle.

Waffle who?

It's waffle that you still haven't opened the door!

Knock, knock.

Who's there?

Noah.

Noah who?

Noah good place to eat?

Knock, knock.

Who's there?

Sultan.

Sultan who?

Sultan pepper.

Knock, knock.

Who's there?

Dill.

Dill who?

Good-bye dill we meet again.

Girl Giggles: A-L

Knock, knock.

Who's there?

Abby.

Abby who?

Abby stung me on my nose.

Knock, knock.
Who's there?
Adelia.
Adelia who?
Adelia the cards after you cut the deck.

Knock, knock.
Who's there?
Adeline.
Adeline who?
You should Adeline to your drawing of the African savanna.

Knock, knock.
Who's there?
Agatha.
Agatha who?
Agatha headache. Do you have an aspirin?

Knock, knock.
Who's there?
Alison.
Alison who?
Alison to you if you listen to me!

Knock, knock.
Who's there?
Alma.
Alma who?
Alma knock-knock jokes are really funny!

Knock, knock.
Who's there?
Althea.
Althea who?
Althea later, dude.

Hi

Knock, knock.
Who's there?
Amanda.
Amanda who?
Amanda fix the refrigerator is here.

73

Knock, knock.
Who's there?
Amy.
Amy who?
Amy-fraid I've forgotten.

Knock, knock.
Who's there?
Anna.
Anna who?
Anna one, Anna two,
Anna three!

Knock, knock.
Who's there?
Annette.
Annette who?
Annette to use the
bathroom, so please
open the door!

Knock, knock.
Who's there?
Annie.
Annie who?
Annie thing I can do to help you?

Knock, knock.
Who's there?
Avery.
Avery who?
Avery time I come to see you we go through this.

Knock, knock.
Who's there?
Barbara.
Barbara who?
"Barbara black sheep, have you any wool . . . ?"

Knock, knock.
Who's there?
Bea.
Bea who?
Bea-cause I like you, I came to visit!

Knock, knock.
Who's there?
Beth.
Beth who?
I didn't sneeze!

Knock, knock.
Who's there?
Betty.
Betty who?
I Betty doesn't know who this is!

Knock, knock.
Who's there?
Betty Bee Bell Grace.
Betty Bee Bell Grace who?
Seriously, how many Betty Bee Bell
Graces do you know?

Knock, knock.
Who's there?
Bonnie.
Bonnie who?
It's Bonnie long time since I've seen you.

Knock, knock.
Who's there?
Brett.
Brett who?
Brett you don't know who this is!

Knock, knock.
Who's there?
Candice.
Candice who?
Candice be true?

Knock, knock.
Who's there?
Carlotta.
Carlotta who?
Carlotta trouble
when it breaks down.

Knock, knock.
Who's there?
Carmen.
Carmen who?
Carmen get it.

Knock, knock.
Who's there?
Carrie.
Carrie who?
Carrie my books for me?

Knock, knock.
Who's there?
Carson.
Carson who?
Carson the freeway drive really fast.

Knock, knock.

Who's there?

Cathy.

Cathy who?

Cathy anything with this blindfold on!

Knock, knock.

Who's there?

Cecile.

Cecile who?

Cecile this envelope before you mail it.

Knock, knock.
Who's there?
Celeste.
Celeste who?
Celeste time I lend you anything!

Knock, knock.
Who's there?
Claire.
Claire who?
Claire the way, I'm coming through!

Knock, knock.
Who's there?
Colleen.
Colleen who?
Colleen up your room. It's a mess!

Knock, knock.
Who's there?
Collette.
Collette who?
Collette crazy, but I'd like to come in and see you.

Knock, knock.
Who's there?
Cynthia.
Cynthia who?
Cynthia been away, I've missed you.

Knock, knock.
Who's there?
Daisy.
Daisy who?
Daisy plays; nights he sleeps.

Knock, knock.
Who's there?
Danielle.
Danielle who?
Danielle at me—it's not my fault.

Knock, knock.
Who's there?
Dawn.
Dawn who?
Dawn do anything I wouldn't do.

Knock, knock.
Who's there?
Della.
Della who?
Sure, I'll Della-nother knock-knock joke!

Knock, knock.

Who's there?

Denise.

Denise who?

Denise are above de ankles.

Knock, knock.
Who's there?
Diane.
Diane who?
I'm Diane to meet you.

Knock, knock.
Who's there?
Eileen.
Eileen who?
Eileen over to tie my shoes.

Knock, knock.
Who's there?
Elizabeth.
Elizabeth who?
Elizabeth of knowledge is a
dangerous thing.

Knock, knock.
Who's there?
Elsie.
Elsie who?
Elsie you later!

Knock, knock.
Who's there?
Erin.
Erin who?
I have to run a quick Erin, but I'll be back!

Knock, knock.
Who's there?
Erma.
Erma who?
"Erma a little teapot, short and stout . . ."

Knock, knock.
Who's there?
Esther.
Esther who?
Esther anything I can do for you?

Knock, knock.
Who's there?
Eve.
Eve who?
Eve me alone!

Knock, knock.
Who's there?
Evie.
Evie who?
Evie wonder why I'm knocking at the door?

Knock, knock.
Who's there?
Faith.
Faith who?
Time to Faith the music.

Knock, knock.
Who's there?
Francie.
Francie who?
Francie meeting you here.

Knock, knock.
Who's there?
Ginny.
Ginny who?
Ginny a hug.

Knock, knock.

Who's there?

Gretel.

Gretel who?

Gretel long, little doggie.

Knock, knock.

Who's there?

Gwen.

Gwen who?

Gwen do you think we can get together?

Knock, knock.

Who's there?

Hailey.

Hailey who?

Hailey cab so I can go home.

Knock, knock.
Who's there?
Hannah.
Hannah who?
Hannah me some of those apples. I'm hungry!

Knock, knock.
Who's there?
Harriet.
Harriet who?
Harriet up—we're late.

Knock, knock.
Who's there?
Henrietta.
Henrietta who?
Henrietta bug
and now he's sick.

Knock, knock.
Who's there?
Ida.
Ida who?
Ida terrible time getting here.

Knock, knock.
Who's there?
Ilona.
Ilona who?
Ilona Ranger.

Knock, knock.
Who's there?
Ima.
Ima who?
Ima waiting to hear another
knock-knock joke.

Knock, knock.
Who's there?
Imogen.
Imogen who?
Imogen life without ice cream.

Knock, knock.
Who's there?
Iris.
Iris who?
Iris I could get a puppy!

Knock, knock.
Who's there?
Isabelle.
Isabelle who?
Isabelle on the cat's collar?

Knock, knock.
Who's there?
Izzy.
Izzy who?
Izzy come, Izzy go.

Knock, knock.
Who's there?
Jess.
Jess who?
I give up—who?

Knock, knock.
Who's there?
Jo.
Jo who?
Jo King!

Knock, knock.
Who's there?
Joan.
Joan who?
Joan call us—we'll call you.

Knock, knock.
Who's there?
Johanna.
Johanna who?
Johanna come out and play?

        Knock, knock.
        Who's there?
        Juana.
        Juana who?
        Juana see a movie tonight?

Knock, knock.
Who's there?
Judith.
Judith who?
Judith thought these knock-knock jokes would get old,
but they don't!

        Knock, knock.
        Who's there?
        Julie.
        Julie who?
        Why don't Julie me alone?

Knock, knock.
Who's there?
Kay.
Kay who?
Kay comes after J.

Knock, knock.
Who's there?
Kim.
Kim who?
I Kim too late for the movie.

Knock, knock.
Who's there?
Lana.
Lana who?
This is the Lana the free.

Knock, knock.
Who's there?
Lauren.
Lauren who?
Lauren order.

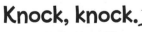

Knock, knock.
Who's there?
Leah.
Leah who?
Leah the door unlocked next time!

Knock, knock.
Who's there?
Lena.
Lena who?
Lena little closer—I have something
to tell you.

Knock, knock.

Who's there?

Linda.

Linda who?

Linda hand! I can't do it all by myself!

Knock, knock.

Who's there?

Lisa.

Lisa who?

Lisa you can do is let me in.

Cat and Dog Crackups

Knock, knock.

Who's there?

A bonus.

A bonus who?

A bonus what a dog likes to chew.

Knock, knock.

Who's there?

Detail.

Detail who?

Detail of de cat is on de end.

Knock, knock.

Who's there?

Cattle.

Cattle who?

Cattle usually purr if you pet her.

Knock, knock.

Who's there?

Patsy.

Patsy who?

Patsy dog on the head. He likes it!

Knock, knock.
Who's there?
Beagle.
Beagle who?
Beagle with cream cheese.

Knock, knock.
Who's there?
Collie.
Collie who?
Collie-flower is good for you.

Knock, knock.
Who's there?
Senior.
Senior who?
Senior dog digging in the trash yesterday.

Knock, knock.
Who's there?
Aware.
Aware who?
Aware, aware has my little dog gone?

Knock, knock.
Who's there?
Feline.
Feline who?
I'm feline fine, thanks.

Knock, knock.
Who's there?
Pooch.
Pooch who?
Pooch your coat on—it's cold outside.

Knock, knock.
Who's there?
Me.
Me who?
You sure have a funny-sounding cat.

Knock, knock.
Who's there?
Bow.
Bow who?
Not bow who, bow wow!

Knock, knock.
Who's there?
Defense.
Defense who?
Defense has a hole in it—
that's how our dog got loose.

Knock, knock.
Who's there?
Champ.
Champ who?
Champ-oo your dog—he's muddy!

Knock, knock.
Who's there?
Landon.
Landon who?
Landon their feet is what cats do.

Knock, knock.
Who's there?
Fido.
Fido who?
Fido known you were sick, I would have brought soup.

Knock, knock.
Who's there?
Sheena.
Sheena who?
Sheena lost dog around here?

Knock, knock.

Who's there?

Neil.

Neil who?

Neil down and pet the cat before
he scratches you!

Knock, knock.

Who's there?

Ken.

Ken who?

Ken you walk my dog for me?

Knock, knock.

Who's there?

Poodle.

Poodle who?

Poodle little mustard on my hot dog.

Knock, knock.
Who's there?
Farmer.
Farmer who?
I hope I get a cat farmer birthday.

Knock, knock.
Who's there?
Flea.
Flea who?
Flea from that dog before he bites you!

Musical Mirth

Knock, knock.

Who's there?

Turnip.

Turnip who?

Turnip the volume—it's my favorite song!

Knock, knock.

Who's there?

Tuna.

Tuna who?

Tuna piano, and it'll sound better.

Knock, knock.

Who's there?

Fiddle.

Fiddle who?

Fiddle make you happy, I'll tell you!

Knock, knock.

Who's there?

Accordion.

Accordion who?

Accordion to the news, it's going
to be sunny today.

Knock, knock.
Who's there?
Sing.
Sing who?
Whoooooooo!

Knock, knock.
Who's there?
Guitar.
Guitar who?
Let's guitar coats—it's cold outside.

Knock, knock.
Who's there?
Duet.
Duet who?
Duet yourself and quit bothering me!

Knock, knock.
Who's there?
Cello.
Cello who?
Cello there!

Knock, knock.
Who's there?
Rupert.
Rupert who?
"Rupert your left foot in; Rupert your left foot out."

Knock, knock.
Who's there?
Shelby.
Shelby who?
"Shelby comin' round the mountain when she comes!"

Knock, knock.
Who's there?
Clarinet.
Clarinet who?
Clarinet-ted a fish, and now she's throwing it back!

Knock, knock.
Who's there?
Jamaica.
Jamaica who?
Jamaica great keyboard player!

Knock, knock.
Who's there?
Abandon.
Abandon who?
Abandon the street is marching this way.

Knock, knock.
Who's there?
Tuba.
Tuba who?
Tuba toothpaste.

      Knock, knock.
      Who's there?
      Rhoda.
      Rhoda who?
      "Row, row, Rhoda boat gently down the
      stream . . ."

Knock, knock.
Who's there?
Rapper.
Rapper who?
Rapper up a sandwich to go.

      Knock, knock.
      Who's there?
      Sonata.
      Sonata who?
      Don't worry, sonata a big deal.

Knock, knock.

Who's there?

Little old lady.

Little old lady who?

Wow—I didn't know you could yodel!

Knock, knock.

Who's there?

Whom.

Whom who?

"Whom, whom on the range, where the deer and the antelope play . . ."

Knock, knock.
Who's there?
Jaws.
Jaws who?
Jaws stopped by to see if you
want to go swimming.

Knock, knock.
Who's there?
General Lee.
General Lee who?
General Lee I do not tell knock-knock jokes.

Knock, knock.
Who's there?
Tarzan.
Tarzan who?
Tarzan stripes forever.

Knock, knock.
Who's there?
Kermit.
Kermit who?
Kermit a crime, and the police will arrest you.

Knock, knock.
Who's there?
King Tut.
King Tut who?
King Tut-key Fried Chicken.

Knock, knock.
Who's there?
Tinker Bell.
Tinker Bell who?
Tinker Bell is out of order.

Knock, knock.
Who's there?
Vivaldi.
Vivaldi who?
Vivaldi homework I have,
I'll be up all night.

Knock, knock.
Who's there?
Yoda.
Yoda who?
Yoda man! Let's hang out more.

Knock, knock.
Who's there?
Alison.
Alison who?
Alison Wonderland.

Knock, knock.
Who's there?
Aladdin.
Aladdin who?
Aladdin the street wants to talk to you.

Knock, knock.
Who's there?
Chimney.
Chimney who?
Chimney Cricket. Have you seen Pinocchio?

Knock, knock.
Who's there?
Eisenhower.
Eisenhower who?
Eisenhower late getting here.

Knock, knock.
Who's there?
Kendall.
Kendall who?
Kendall and Barbie go together.

Knock, knock.
Who's there?
Ben Hur.
Ben Hur who?
Ben Hur for a while now, can you let me in?

Knock, knock.
Who's there?
Darwin.
Darwin who?
I'll be Darwin you open the door.

Knock, knock.
Who's there?
Mozart.
Mozart who?
Mozart is found in museums.

Knock, knock.
Who's there?
Gandhi.
Gandhi who?
Gandhi kids come out and play?

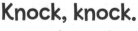

Knock, knock.
Who's there?
Ivory.
Ivory who?
Ivory strong, like Tarzan!

Knock, knock.

Who's there?

Scissor.

Scissor who?

Scissor and Cleopatra.

Knock, knock.

Who's there?

Sherlock.

Sherlock who?

Sherlock the door. See if I care.

Knock, knock.

Who's there?

Snow.

Snow who?

No, Snow What and the Seven Dwarfs.

Knock, knock.

Who's there?

Rockefeller.

Rockefeller who?

Rockefeller in his cradle and he'll go right to sleep.

Knock, knock.

Who's there?

Gravy.

Gravy who?

Gravy Crockett.

Knock, knock.

Who's there?

Caesar.

Caesar who?

Caesar quickly before she gets away!

Knock, knock.

Who's there?

Bill Gates.

Bill Gates who?

Bill Gates a bike for his birthday.

Knock, knock.
Who's there?
Churchill.
Churchill who?
Churchill be held on Sunday.

Knock, knock.
Who's there?
Thor.
Thor who?
Thor-ry, wrong door.

Boy Belly Laughs: A-L

Knock, knock.
Who's there?
Abe.
Abe who?
Abe C D E F G . . .

Knock, knock.
Who's there?
Abner.
Abner who?
Abner-noon, pardner.

Knock, knock.
Who's there?
Adam.
Adam who?
Adam up and tell me the total.

Knock, knock.
Who's there?
Adolf.
Adolf who?
Adolf ball hit me in
the mowf.

Knock, knock.
Who's there?
Al.
Al who?
Al show you who's boss!

Knock, knock.
Who's there?
Alastair.
Alastair who?
Alastair at you if you stare at me.

Knock, knock.
Who's there?
Alfie.
Alfie who?
Alfie you tomorrow!

Knock, knock.
Who's there?
Allen.
Allen who?
Allen a day's work.

Knock, knock.
Who's there?
Alvin.
Alvin who?
Alvin a great time, how about you?

Knock, knock.
Who's there?
Andy.
Andy who?
Andy-body want to go to the movies?

Knock, knock.
Who's there?
Arnold.
Arnold who?
Arnold friend you haven't seen for years.

Knock, knock.
Who's there?
Art.
Art who?
Art-2 D-2. May the force be with you!

Knock, knock.
Who's there?
Barry.
Barry who?
Barry glad to see you.

Knock, knock.
Who's there?
Ben.
Ben who?
Ben knocking on this door all morning.

Knock, knock.
Who's there?
Benny.
Benny who?
Benny thing happening with you today?

Knock, knock.
Who's there?
Braden.
Braden who?
Braden my hair for the big recital!

Knock, knock.
Who's there?
Brent.
Brent who?
Brent out of shape.

Knock, knock.
Who's there?
Bruce.
Bruce who?
I have a Bruce on my shin.

Knock, knock.
Who's there?
Byron.
Byron who?
There's a Byron, get one free sale at the mall!

Knock, knock.
Who's there?
Carl.
Carl who?
Carl get you there faster than a bike.

Knock, knock.
Who's there?
Chester.
Chester who?
Chester ordinary door-to-door salesman.

Knock, knock.
Who's there?
Colin.
Colin who?
Just Colin to tell you another great knock-knock joke.

Knock, knock.
Who's there?
Dale.
Dale who?
Dale come when you call.

Knock, knock.
Who's there?
Darren.
Darren who?
I'm Darren you to tell a funnier knock-knock joke.

Knock, knock.
Who's there?
Darryl.
Darryl who?
Darryl never be another you.

Knock, knock.
Who's there?
Dewey.
Dewey who?
Dewey get to hear more knock-knock jokes?

Knock, knock.
Who's there?
Diego.
Diego who?
Diego before de B.

Knock, knock.
Who's there?
Doug.
Doug who?
I Doug deep and still couldn't find
my keys. Please let me in!

Knock, knock.
Who's there?
Douglas.
Douglas who?
Douglas is broken—
don't cut yourself.

Knock, knock.
Who's there?
Dwight.
Dwight who?
There's Dwight way and there's de wrong way.

Knock, knock.
Who's there?
Earl.
Earl who?
Earl to bed, Earl to rise.

Knock, knock.
Who's there?
Eddie.
Eddie who?
Eddie body home?

Knock, knock.
Who's there?
Ethan.
Ethan who?
You are Ethan me out of houth and home.

Knock, knock.
Who's there?
Ewan.
Ewan who?
No, it's just me!

Knock, knock.
Who's there?
Ezra.
Ezra who?
Ezra no hope for me?

Knock, knock.
Who's there?
Ferris.
Ferris who?
Ferris fair, so don't cheat.

Knock, knock.
Who's there?
Fitzwilliam.
Fitzwilliam who?
Fitzwilliam better than it
fits me.

Knock, knock.
Who's there?
Frank.
Frank who?
Frank you for being my friend.

Knock, knock.
Who's there?
Frasier.
Frasier who?
Frasier going to have to let me in sometime!

Knock, knock.
Who's there?
Freddie.
Freddie who?
Freddie or not, here I come.

Knock, knock.
Who's there?
Gabe.
Gabe who?
I Gabe it everything I've got.

Knock, knock.
Who's there?
Galway.
Galway who?
Galway and leave me alone.

Knock, knock.
Who's there?
Gary.
Gary who?
Gary me inside—my legs are tired.

Knock, knock.
Who's there?
Gino.
Gino who?
Gino, these knock-knock jokes are
kind of fun.

Knock, knock.
Who's there?
Gus.
Gus who?
That's what *you're* supposed to do.

Knock, knock.
Who's there?
Hal.
Hal who?
Halloo to you, too!

Knock, knock.
Who's there?
Hank.
Hank who?
You're welcome.

Knock, knock.
Who's there?
Hans.
Hans who?
Hans up—you're under arrest!

Knock, knock.
Who's there?
Harold.
Harold who?
I'm eleven—Harold are you?

Knock, knock.
Who's there?
Harry.
Harry who?
Harry up and open the door!

Knock, knock.
Who's there?
Hiram.
Hiram who?
Hiram fine, how are you?

Knock, knock.
Who's there?
Howard.
Howard who?
Howard you doing today?

Knock, knock.
Who's there?
Howie.
Howie who?
Howie going to figure this out?

Knock, knock.
Who's there?
Hugo.
Hugo who?
Hugo first and I'll go second.

Knock, knock.
Who's there?
Ivan.
Ivan who?
"Ivan working on the
railroad . . ."

Knock, knock.
Who's there?
Ivor.
Ivor who?
Ivor sore hand from knocking on this door.

Knock, knock.
Who's there?
Jacob.
Jacob who?
Jacob your mind! Do you want to hear another knock-knock joke?

Knock, knock.
Who's there?
Jeff.
Jeff who?
Jeff in one ear, please speak up!

Knock, knock.
Who's there?
Jess.
Jess who?
Jess me and my shadow.

Knock, knock.
Who's there?
Jimmy.
Jimmy who?
Jimmy a chance, will you?

Knock, knock.
Who's there?
John.
John who?
John me for dinner?

Knock, knock.
Who's there?
José.
José who?
"José, can you see . . . ?"

Knock, knock.
Who's there?
Justin.
Justin who?
Justin town . . . thought I'd say hi!

Knock, knock.
Who's there?
Keith.
Keith who?
Keith away from the edge!

Knock, knock.
Who's there?
Ken.
Ken who?
Ken I come in? It's freezing out here!

Knock, knock.
Who's there?
Kenneth.
Kenneth who?
Kenneth little kid play with you?

Knock, knock.
Who's there?
Kent.
Kent who?
Kent you tell by my voice?

Knock, knock.
Who's there?
Leif.
Leif who?
Leif me alone.

Knock, knock.
Who's there?
Len.
Len who?
Len me five bucks for lunch?

Knock, knock.
Who's there?
Leon.
Leon who?
Leon me when you're not strong.

Knock, knock.
Who's there?
Les.
Les who?
Les one there is a rotten egg!

Knock, knock.
Who's there?
Lionel.
Lionel who?
**Lionel always get you in trouble,
so tell the truth!**

Knock, knock.

Who's there?

Logan.

Logan who?

Logan see if there's a full moon out.

Knock, knock.

Who's there?

Lucas.

Lucas who?

Lucas in the eye and tell us you don't want to hear another knock-knock joke!

Knock, knock.

Who's there?

Luke.

Luke who?

Luke before you leap.

Knock, knock.

Who's there?

Candy.

Candy who?

Candy cow jump over
de moon?

Knock, knock.
Who's there?
Diesel.
Diesel who?
Diesel be the best cookies ever.

Knock, knock.
Who's there?
Ben and Anna.
Ben and Anna who?
Ben and Anna split—they're gone.

Knock, knock.
Who's there?
Achoo.
Achoo who?
Achoo my gum every day.

Knock, knock.
Who's there?
Howdy.
Howdy who?
Howdy-licious is this pie?

Knock, knock.
Who's there?
I-8.
I-8 who?
I-8 lunch already, but I'd take some dessert!

Knock, knock.
Who's there?
Ice-cream soda.
Ice-cream soda who?
ICE-CREAM SODA WHOLE
WORLD CAN HEAR ME!

Knock, knock.
Who's there?
Felix.
Felix who?
Felix my ice cream again, he'll be in trouble.

Knock, knock.
Who's there?
Gel-O.
Gel-O who?
Gel-O, it's me again.

Knock, knock.
Who's there?
Dee.
Dee who?
Dee cake is in dee oven.

Knock, knock.
Who's there?
Effie.
Effie who?
Effie'd known you were coming, he'd have baked a cake.

Knock, knock.
Who's there?
Grover.
Grover who?
Grover there and get me a cookie, please.

Knock, knock.
Who's there?
Cola.
Cola who?
Cola doctor. My stomach hurts.

Knock, knock.

Who's there?

Duncan.

Duncan who?

Duncan cookies in milk tastes good.

Knock, knock.

Who's there?

Truffle.

Truffle who?

What's the truffle with you?

Knock, knock.

Who's there?

Mint.

Mint who?

I mint to tell you sooner.

Knock, knock.
Who's there?
Oswald.
Oswald who?
Oswald my bubble gum.

—Gulp!

Knock, knock.
Who's there?
Lemmy.
Lemmy who?
Lemmy have another cookie, please.

Knock, knock.
Who's there?
Soda.
Soda who?
Soda answer is still no?

Knock, knock.
Who's there?
Handsome.
Handsome who?
Handsome of those cookies over, please.
I'm hungry!

Knock, knock.
Who's there?
Harriet.
Harriet who?
Harriet so much ice cream he got sick to
his stomach.

Knock, knock.
Who's there?
Pudding.
Pudding who?
Pudding on your shoes
before your pants is a
bad idea.

Knock, knock.
Who's there?
Arthur.
Arthur who?
Arthur any cookies left? I could use a snack!

Knock, knock.
Who's there?
Lois.
Lois who?
Lois shelf is where I keep the cookies.

Knock, knock.
Who's there?
Icing.
Icing who?
Icing in the shower every morning.

Knock, knock.
Who's there?
Doughnut.
Doughnut who?
Doughnut make you laugh when people
tell knock-knock jokes?

Household Humor

Knock, knock.
Who's there?
A broken pencil.
A broken pencil who?
Oh, never mind, it's pointless.

Knock, knock.
Who's there?
Hanover.
Hanover who?
Hanover the remote control, please.

Knock, knock.
Who's there?
Comb.
Comb who?
Comb out and play with me.

Knock, knock.
Who's there?
One shoe.
One shoe who?
One shoe let me in?

Knock, knock.
Who's there?
Razor.
Razor who?
Razor hand if you know the answer.

Knock, knock.
Who's there?
Needle.
Needle who?
Needle little help with your homework?

Knock, knock.
Who's there?
Dime.
Dime who?
Dime to go to bed.

Knock, knock.
Who's there?
Aaron.
Aaron who?
The Aaron here is a little stuffy. Could you open a window?

Knock, knock.
Who's there?
Couch.
Couch who?
Couch me if you can!

Knock, knock.

Who's there?

Wheelbarrow.

Wheelbarrow who?

Wheelbarrow some money from Mom and Dad.

Knock, knock.
Who's there?
Gauze.
Gauze who?
Gauze it's important to exercise.

Knock, knock.
Who's there?
Radio.
Radio who?
Radio not, here I come!

Knock, knock.
Who's there?
Mild.
Mild who?
Mild bike was red but my new bike is blue.

Knock, knock.
Who's there?
Dwayne.
Dwayne who?
Dwayne the bathtub—I'm dwowning.

Knock, knock.
Who's there?
Underwear.
Underwear who?
I underwear I left my shoes.

Knock, knock.
Who's there?
Albie.
Albie who?
Albie upstairs if you need anything!

Knock, knock.
Who's there?
Button.
Button who?
Button in is not polite.

Knock, knock.
Who's there?
Desiree.
Desiree who?
Desiree of sunshine coming through my window!

Knock, knock.

Who's there?

Sandal.

Sandal who?

Sandal stick to your legs if you get them wet.

Knock, knock.

Who's there?

Dishes.

Dishes who?

Dishes a very bad joke!

Knock, knock.

Who's there?

Amigo.

Amigo who?

Amigo to bed now, I'm tired.

Knock, knock.
Who's there?
Despair.
Despair who?
Despair tire is flat.

Knock, knock.
Who's there?
Tire.
Tire who?
Tire shoe before you trip!

Knock, knock.
Who's there?
Wok.
Wok who?
I wok all the way here and you won't even let me come in!

Knock, knock.
Who's there?
Alfred.
Alfred who?
Alfred the needle if you sew the buttons.

Knock, knock.
Who's there?
Mikey.
Mikey who?
Mikey won't fit in this lock.

Knock, knock.
Who's there?
Deluxe.
Deluxe who?
Deluxe-smith. I'm here to fix de lock.

Knock, knock.
Who's there?
Ammonia.
Ammonia who?
Ammonia going to tell you once, so
listen carefully.

Knock, knock.
Who's there?
Distress.
Distress who?
Distress was on sale. Do you like it?

Knock, knock.
Who's there?
Pizza.
Pizza who?
Pizza the puzzle is missing.

Knock, knock.
Who's there?
Pasture.
Pasture who?
Pasture bedtime, isn't it?

Knock, knock.
Who's there?
Arthur.
Arthur who?
Arthur-mometer is broken.

Knock, knock.
Who's there?
Ammon.
Ammon who?
Ammon old hand at fixing things.

Knock, knock.
Who's there?
Lego.
Lego who?
Lego of the doorknob so I can come in!

Knock, knock.
Who's there?
Michael.
Michael who?
I Michael you on the phone later.

Knock, knock.
Who's there?
Unit.
Unit who?
Unit me such a beautiful scarf!

Knock, knock.
Who's there?
Andrew.
Andrew who?
Andrew on the wall, and
boy is she in trouble!

Knock, knock.
Who's there?
Noel.
Noel who?
Noel bows on the table, please.

Knock, knock.
Who's there?
Dragon.
Dragon who?
Dragon easy chair over here
and let's talk.

Knock, knock.
Who's there?
Anita.
Anita who?
Anita tissue.

Knock, knock.
Who's there?
Tish.
Tish who?
Why, yes, I'd love a tissue.

Knock, knock.
Who's there?
House.
House who?
House it going for you?

Knock, knock.
Who's there?
Goliath.
Goliath who?
Goliath down. You looketh tired.

Knock, knock.
Who's there?
Atlas.
Atlas who?
Atlas, it's the weekend!

Knock, knock.
Who's there?
Clothesline.
Clothesline who?
Clothesline all over the floor
end up wrinkled.

Knock, knock.
Who's there?
Harmony.
Harmony who?
Harmony times do I have to tell you to clean your room?

Knock, knock.
Who's there?
Bed.
Bed who?
Bed you can't guess
who I am.

Knock, knock.
Who's there?
Window.
Window who?
Window we eat?

Knock, knock.
Who's there?
Winnie.
Winnie who?
Winnie gets home, you can ask him.

Knock, knock.
Who's there?
Garden.
Garden who?
Garden my gold
from pirates.

Knock, knock.
Who's there?
Hallways.
Hallways who?
Why are you hallways late?

Knock, knock.

Who's there?

Juicy.

Juicy who?

Juicy any monsters under my bed?

Knock, knock.

Who's there?

Esau.

Esau who?

Esau him come in through the window.

Knock, knock.

Who's there?

Thermos.

Thermos who?

Thermos be a better way.

Knock, knock.
Who's there?
Sofa.
Sofa who?
Sofa so good.

Knock, knock.
Who's there?
Electra.
Electra who?
Electra-city. Isn't that
shocking?

Knock, knock.
Who's there?
Isabelle.
Isabelle who?
Isabelle on your house working?

Knock, knock.
Who's there?
Gwenna.
Gwenna who?
Gwenna phone rings, answer it!

Knock, knock.

Who's there?

Jester.

Jester who?

Jester minute—I'm trying to find my keys.

Knock, knock.

Who's there?

Funnel.

Funnel who?

The funnel start once you let me in!

Knock, knock.
Who's there?
Biggish.
Biggish who?
No, thanks, I'll take the smallest shoe.

Knock, knock.
Who's there?
July.
July who?
July to me about stealing
my piggy bank?

Knock, knock.
Who's there?
Rufus.
Rufus who?
Rufus leaking, and I'm getting wet!

Knock, knock.
Who's there?
Diploma.
Diploma who?
Diploma to fix da leak.

Knock, knock.
Who's there?
Delta.
Delta who?
Delta great hand of cards.

Knock, knock.
Who's there?
Disk.
Disk who?
Disk is a recorded message.

Knock, knock.
Who's there?
Hurley.
Hurley who?
Hurley to bed, Hurley to rise.

Knock, knock.
Who's there?
Dishes.
Dishes who?
Dishes not the end of my
knock-knock jokes!

Holiday Ha-Has

Knock, knock.
Who's there?
Twig.
Twig who?
Twig or tweat!

Knock, knock.

Who's there?

Hair combs.

Hair combs who?

"Hair combs Santa Claus, right down Santa Claus Lane!"

Knock, knock.

Who's there?

Ivan.

Ivan who?

Ivan to go trick-or-treating!

Knock, knock.
Who's there?
Irish.
Irish who?
Irish you a Merry Christmas!

Knock, knock.
Who's there?
Osborne.
Osborne who?
Osborne today. It's my birthday.

Knock, knock.
Who's there?
Abbie.
Abbie who?
Abbie birthday!

Knock, knock.
Who's there?
Honey.
Honey who?
Honey-kah is my favorite holiday!

Knock, knock.

Who's there?

Delight.

Delight who?

Delight coming from the menorah is beautiful.

Knock, knock.

Who's there?

Mary and Abby.

Mary and Abby who?

Mary Christmas and Abby New Year!

Knock, knock.

Who's there?

Ditty.

Ditty who?

Ditty see Santa Claus or not?

Knock, knock.
Who's there?
Dexter.
Dexter who?
"Dexter halls with boughs of holly!"

Knock, knock.
Who's there?
Mayor.
Mayor who?
Mayor Kwanzaa be filled with peace and unity!

Knock, knock.
Who's there?
Bertha.
Bertha who?
Bertha-day greetings to you!

Knock, knock.
Who's there?
Dispatch.
Dispatch who?
Dispatch of pumpkins is huge!

Knock, knock.
Who's there?
Howl.
Howl who?
Howl you be dressing up for Halloween this year?

Knock, knock.
Who's there?
Doughnut.
Doughnut who?
Doughnut open this
until your birthday.

Knock, knock.
Who's there?
Honda.
Honda who?
"Honda first day of Christmas, my true love gave to me . . ."

Knock, knock.
Who's there?
Hannah.
Hannah who?
"Hannah partridge in a pear tree . . ."

Knock, knock.
Who's there?
Huff.
Huff who?
Huff you heard the news? Santa Claus is coming to town!

Knock, knock.
Who's there?
Esther.
Esther who?
Esther Bunny.

Knock, knock.
Who's there?
Stella.
Stella who?
Stella-nother Esther Bunny.

Knock, knock.
Who's there?
Megan and chicken.
Megan and chicken who?
"He's Megan a list and chicken it twice, he's gonna find out who's naughty or nice. . . ."

Knock, knock.
Who's there?
Value.
Value who?
Value be my Valentine?

Knock, knock.
Who's there?
Isolate.
Isolate who?
Isolate to the Valentine's Day party—I almost missed it!

Knock, knock.
Who's there?
Latke.
Latke who?
Latke be said about Hanukkah!

Knock, knock.
Who's there?
Yule.
Yule who?
Yule never know who it is unless you open the door!

Knock, knock.
Who's there?
Murray.
Murray who?
Murray Christmas to all, and to all
a good night!

Girl Giggles: M-Z

Knock, knock.

Who's there?

Mabel.

Mabel who?

Mabel isn't working right either.

Knock, knock.
Who's there?
Madison.
Madison who?
Madison is good to take when you're sick.

Knock, knock.
Who's there?
Mae.
Mae who?
Mae-be I'll tell you, and Mae-be I won't.

Knock, knock.
Who's there?
Mandy.
Mandy who?
Mandy lifeboats—de ship is sinking.

Knock, knock.
Who's there?
Mara.
Mara who?
"Mara, Mara on the wall . . ."

Knock, knock.
Who's there?
Marietta.
Marietta who?
Marietta whole cake.

Knock, knock.
Who's there?
Marilee.
Marilee who?
"Marilee, Marilee, Marilee, life is but a dream!"

Knock, knock.
Who's there?
Marsha.
Marsha who?
Marshamallow.

Knock, knock.
Who's there?
Mary.
Mary who?
Mary me, please!
I love you!

Knock, knock.
Who's there?
Maura.
Maura who?
The Maura the merrier.

Knock, knock.
Who's there?
Maya.
Maya who?
Maya hand is hurting from all this knocking.
Will you please let me in?

Knock, knock.
Who's there?
Meg.
Meg who?
Meg up your mind.

Knock, knock.

Who's there?

Megan.

Megan who?

You're Megan me crazy with all these knock-knock jokes.

Knock, knock.

Who's there?

Mimi.

Mimi who?

Mimi! Me! Me! It's *me*—how many more times do I have to tell you?

Knock, knock.

Who's there?

Minnie.

Minnie who?

Minnie more miles to go.

Knock, knock.
Who's there?
Morgan.
Morgan who?
Morgan I expected.

Knock, knock.
Who's there?
Nadia.
Nadia who?
Nadia head if you understand what
I'm saying.

Knock, knock.
Who's there?
Nicole.
Nicole who?
I'll give you a Nicole if you let me in.

Knock, knock.

Who's there?

Olive.

Olive who?

Olive you so much!

Knock, knock.

Who's there?

Peg.

Peg who?

Peg your pardon—I've got the wrong door.

Knock, knock.

Who's there?

Petunia.

Petunia who?

There's a problem Petunia and me.

Knock, knock.
Who's there?
Phyllis.
Phyllis who?
Phyllis in on all the news.

Knock, knock.
Who's there?
Quincy.
Quincy who?
You Quincy the doctor now.

Knock, knock.
Who's there?
Riley.
Riley who?
Riley makes up his mind, let's play a game.

Knock, knock.
Who's there?
Rita.
Rita who?
Rita book. It's fun!

Knock, knock.
Who's there?
Rosa.
Rosa who?
Rosa corn grow in the field.

Knock, knock.
Who's there?
Roxanne.
Roxanne who?
Roxanne coral make the aquarium look nice.

Knock, knock.
Who's there?
Ruth.
Ruth who?
The Ruth of the matter is, I like you.

Knock, knock.
Who's there?
Sabina.
Sabina who?
Sabina long time since I've seen you.

Knock, knock.
Who's there?
Sadie.
Sadie who?
If I Sadie magic word will you let me in?

Knock, knock.
Who's there?
Sally.
Sally who?
Sally dance?

Knock, knock.
Who's there?
Samantha.
Samantha who?
Can you give me Samantha to my questions?

Knock, knock.

Who's there?

Sandy.

Sandy who?

Sandy door—I just got a splinter.

Knock, knock.

Who's there?

Sarah.

Sarah who?

Sarah reason you're not laughing?

Knock, knock.

Who's there?

Sasha.

Sasha who?

Sasha fuss, just because I knocked
at your door.

Knock, knock.

Who's there?

Sharon.

Sharon who?

Sharon share alike.

Knock, knock.
Who's there?
Sherri.
Sherri who?
Sherri dance with me?

Knock, knock.
Who's there?
Shirley.
Shirley who?
Shirley I'll tell you another
knock-knock joke.

Knock, knock.
Who's there?
Sophie.
Sophie who?
I'm hungry, Sophie me.

Knock, knock.
Who's there?
Stevie.
Stevie who?
Stevie on? Please turn it off.

Knock, knock.
Who's there?
Sue.
Sue who?
Don't ask me. I'm not your lawyer.

Knock, knock.
Who's there?
Tanya.
Tanya who?
Tanya frown upside-down!

Knock, knock.
Who's there?
Taryn.
Taryn who?
It's Taryn me up inside that you won't let me in!

Knock, knock.
Who's there?
Taylor.
Taylor who?
Taylor little sister to pick
up her toys.

Knock, knock.
Who's there?
Thea.
Thea who?
Thea later, alligator.

Knock, knock.
Who's there?
Theresa.
Theresa who?
Theresa fly in my soup.

Knock, knock.
Who's there?
Tori.
Tori who?
Tori I bumped into you.

Knock, knock.
Who's there?
Uta.
Uta who?
Uta sight, Uta mind.

Knock, knock.

Who's there?

Vera.

Vera who?

Vera few people think these jokes are funny.

Knock, knock.

Who's there?

Viola.

Viola who?

Viola sudden don't you know me?

Knock, knock.
Who's there?
Violet.
Violet who?
Violet that go to waste?

Knock, knock.
Who's there?
Wanda.
Wanda who?
Wanda come out and play?

Knock, knock.
Who's there?
Wendy.
Wendy who?
"Wendy wind blows, de cradle will rock . . ."

Knock, knock.
Who's there?
Wilma.
Wilma who?
Wilma dinner be ready soon?

Knock, knock.
Who's there?
Xena.
Xena who?
Xena good movie lately?

Knock, knock.
Who's there?
Yolanda.
Yolanda who?
Yolanda me some money?

Knock, knock.
Who's there?
Zelda.
Zelda who?
Zelda house—I think
it's haunted!

Knock, knock.
Who's there?
Zizi.
Zizi who?
Zizi when you know how.

Big Bug Laughs

Knock, knock.

Who's there?

Spider.

Spider who?

In spider everything, I still like you.

Knock, knock.
Who's there?
Beehive.
Beehive who?
Beehive yourself or you'll get in trouble.

Knock, knock.
Who's there?
Roach.
Roach who?
Roach you a letter—did you get it?

Knock, knock.
Who's there?
Amos.
Amos who?
Amos-quito bit me.

Knock, knock.
Who's there?
Andy.
Andy who?
Andy bit me again.

Knock, knock.
Who's there?
Honeybee.
Honeybee who?
Honeybee a dear and get me some juice.

Knock, knock.
Who's there?
Flea.
Flea who?
Flea blind mice.

Knock, knock.
Who's there?
Gnats.
Gnats who?
Gnats not a bit funny.

Knock, knock.
Who's there?
Zombies.
Zombies who?
Zombies make honey, and zombies don't.

Knock, knock.
Who's there?
Termites.
Termites who?
Termites the night we're going out.

Knock, knock.
Who's there?
Beezer.
Beezer who?
Beezer black and yellow.

Knock, knock.
Who's there?
Bug spray.
Bug spray who?
Bug spray that snakes and birds will stay away.

Knock, knock.
Who's there?
Wood ant.
Wood ant who?
Don't be afraid. I wood ant hurt a fly!

Knock, knock.
Who's there?
Thumping.
Thumping who?
Thumping green and thlimy is crawling up your leg.

Knock, knock.
Who's there?
Weevil.
Weevil who?
Weevil stay only a few minutes.

Knock, knock.
Who's there?
Grub.
Grub who?
Grub hold of my hand and let's get out of here.

School Sillies

Knock, knock.

Who's there?

Geometry.

Geometry who?

Geometry in the class play, but I
wish I were a flower.

Knock, knock.
Who's there?
Asher.
Asher who?
Asher could use some help with my homework.

Knock, knock.
Who's there?
Norma Lee.
Norma Lee who?
Norma Lee I do my homework after dinner.

Knock, knock.
Who's there?
Justin.
Justin who?
Justin time for recess.

Knock, knock.
Who's there?
Wayne.
Wayne who?
Wayne is the spelling test?

Knock, knock.
Who's there?
Windows.
Windows who?
Windows school start? I don't want to be late!

Knock, knock.
Who's there?
Census.
Census who?
Census Saturday, we don't have to go to school.

Knock, knock.
Who's there?
Conrad.
Conrad who?
Conrad-ulations on your good report card!

Knock, knock.
Who's there?
Les.
Les who?
Les go to the cafeteria.

Knock, knock.
Who's there?
Mister E.
Mister E. who?
Mister E. meat is what
they are serving for
lunch today.

Knock, knock.
Who's there?
Decay.
Decay who?
Decay is after de J in the alphabet song.

Knock, knock.
Who's there?
Ellis.
Ellis who?
Ellis the letter after K and before M.

Knock, knock.
Who's there?
Earl.
Earl who?
Earl be glad when summer vacation starts.

Knock, knock.
Who's there?
Joanne.
Joanne who?
Joanne tell.

Knock, knock.
Who's there?
Benjamin.
Benjamin who?
Benjamin with the school band all day.

Knock, knock.
Who's there?
Degrade.
Degrade who?
Degrade I got on my spelling test wasn't so good.

Knock, knock.
Who's there?
Pause.
Pause who?
Pause your homework in now, please.

Knock, knock.
Who's there?
Don Juan.
Don Juan who?
Don Juan to miss school today.

Knock, knock.
Who's there?
Pencil.
Pencil who?
Pencil fall down if you don't wear a belt.

Knock, knock.
Who's there?
Marcus.
Marcus who?
Marcus both down for the school talent show!

Knock, knock.
Who's there?
Event.
Event who?
Event home sick from school today.

Knock, knock.
Who's there?
Stacey.
Stacey who?
Stacey-ted until the school bus stops.

Knock, knock.
Who's there?
Jewel.
Jewel who?
Jewel be sorry when the principal finds out.

Knock, knock.
Who's there?
Wanda.
Wanda who?
I Wanda where I put my homework.

Knock, knock.
Who's there?
Ketchup.
Ketchup who?
Ketchup or else you'll miss the school bus!

Knock, knock.
Who's there?
Mister.
Mister who?
Mister at the bus stop—do you know where
she is?

Knock, knock.
Who's there?
Spell.
Spell who?
W-H-O.

Knock, knock.
Who's there?
Teachers.
Teachers who?
Teachers (three cheers) for the red,
white, and blue!

Knock, knock.
Who's there?
Sadie.
Sadie who?
Sadie ten times table without any mistakes.

Knock, knock.
Who's there?
Prod.
Prod who?
Prod of you for getting an A.

Knock, knock.
Who's there?
Tamara.
Tamara who?
Tamara is another school day.

Knock, knock.

Who's there?

Rice.

Rice who?

Rice and shine, it's the first day of school!

Boy Belly Laughs: M-Z

Knock, knock.

Who's there?

Manny.

Manny who?

How Manny knock-knock jokes do you want to hear?

Knock, knock.
Who's there?
Manuel.
Manuel who?
Manuel be sorry if you don't let me in.

Knock, knock.
Who's there?
Mark.
Mark who?
Mark my words, you will open this door!

Knock, knock.
Who's there?
Matthew.
Matthew who?
Matthew is pinthing
my foot.

228

Knock, knock.
Who's there?
Max.
Max who?
Max no difference to me!

Knock, knock.
Who's there?
Micah.
Micah who?
Micah has a flat tire—can you help?

Knock, knock.
Who's there?
Moe.
Moe who?
Moe knock-knock jokes, please.

Knock, knock.
Who's there?
Mort.
Mort who?
Mort to the point, who are you?

Knock, knock.

Who's there?

Nick.

Nick who?

You're just in the Nick of time—I was about to tell another knock-knock joke!

Knock, knock.

Who's there?

Noah.

Noah who?

Noah fence but you're asking a lot of questions.

Knock, knock.

Who's there?

Oliver.

Oliver who?

Oliver troubles are over.

Knock, knock.
Who's there?
Omar.
Omar who?
Omar goodness, wrong door!

Knock, knock.
Who's there?
Oscar.
Oscar who?
Oscar silly question, get a silly answer.

Knock, knock.
Who's there?
Otto.
Otto who?
Otto know. I've got amnesia.

Knock, knock.
Who's there?
Owen.
Owen who?
I'm Owen you a lot of money, but I'll pay you back soon!

Knock, knock.
Who's there?
Ozzie.
Ozzie who?
Ozzie you later, alligator.

Knock, knock.
Who's there?
Paul.
Paul who?
Paul up a chair and I'll tell you.

Knock, knock.
Who's there?
Raymond.
Raymond who?
Raymond me to go to the store to get some milk and eggs.

Knock, knock.
Who's there?
Reggie.
Reggie who?
Reggie to open the door yet?

Knock, knock.
Who's there?
Rich.
Rich who?
Rich knock-knock joke is your favorite?

Knock, knock.
Who's there?
Ringo.
Ringo who?
Ringo 'round your finger.

Knock, knock.
Who's there?
Ron.
Ron who?
You can Ron, but you can't hide!

Knock, knock.

Who's there?

Rowan.

Rowan who?

Rowan a boat is hard work.

Knock, knock.

Who's there?

Roy.

Roy who?

"Roy, Roy, Roy your boat, gently down the stream."

Knock, knock.

Who's there?

Russell.

Russell who?

Russell up something good for me to eat.

Knock, knock.

Who's there?

Sam.

Sam who?

Sam person who knocked last time.

Knock, knock.
Who's there?
Scott.
Scott who?
Scott nothing to do with you.

Knock, knock.
Who's there?
Sherwood.
Sherwood who?
Sherwood like some ice cream.

Knock, knock.
Who's there?
Stan.
Stan who?
Stan back. I think I'm going to sneeze.

Knock, knock.
Who's there?
Stu.
Stu who?
Stu late to ask questions.

Knock, knock.
Who's there?
Thatcher.
Thatcher who?
Thatcher idea of a good joke?

Knock, knock.
Who's there?
Thayer.
Thayer who?
Thayer sorry and I'll forgive you.

Knock, knock.
Who's there?
Theodore.
Theodore who?
Theodore is shut—please open it.

Knock, knock.
Who's there?
Tobias.
Tobias who?
Tobias some ice cream, you need some money.

Knock, knock.
Who's there?
Toby.
Toby who?
Toby, or not Toby, that is the question.

Knock, knock.
Who's there?
Tyrone.
Tyrone who?
Tyrone shoelaces.

Knock, knock.
Who's there?
Van.
Van who?
Van can I see you again?

Knock, knock.
Who's there?
Vaughn.
Vaughn who?
Vaughn plus Vaughn equals two.

Knock, knock.
Who's there?
Victor.
Victor who?
Victor his pants when he
bent over.

Knock, knock.
Who's there?
Wade.
Wade who?
Wade a minute—I want to tell you another
knock-knock joke!

Knock, knock.
Who's there?
Walt.
Walt who?
Walt! Who goes there?

Knock, knock.
Who's there?
Walter.
Walter who?
Walter you doing here so early?

Knock, knock.
Who's there?
Warner.
Warner who?
Warner you coming over?

Knock, knock.
Who's there?
Wayne.
Wayne who?
"Wayne, Wayne go away!"

Knock, knock.
Who's there?
Wiley.
Wiley who?
Wiley was sleeping, his alarm clock went off.

Knock, knock.
Who's there?
Will.
Will who?
Will you listen to another
knock-knock joke?

Knock, knock.
Who's there?
William.
William who?
William mind your own business!

Knock, knock.
Who's there?
Willis.
Willis who?
Willis joke make you laugh?

Knock, knock.
Who's there?
Woody.
Woody who?
Woody like to hear another knock-knock joke?

Knock, knock.
Who's there?
Xavier.
Xavier who?
Xavier money
for a rainy day.

Knock, knock.
Who's there?
Zeke.
Zeke who?
Zeke and you shall find . . .

Knock, knock.
Who's there?
Zeus.
Zeus who?
Zeus house is this, anyway?

Family Funnies

Knock, knock.

Who's there?

Aunt Lou.

Aunt Lou who?

Aunt Lou do you think you are?

Knock, knock.

Who's there?

Conner.

Conner who?

Conner sister come out and play?

Knock, knock.

Who's there?

Sour.

Sour who?

Sour your brothers doing these days?

Knock, knock.

Who's there?

Amazon.

Amazon who?

Amazon of a teacher. What does your father do?

Knock, knock.

Who's there?

Aunt Tillie.

Aunt Tillie who?

Aunt Tillie says come in, I'm staying right here.

Knock, knock.
Who's there?
Butternut.
Butternut who?
Butternut forget your father's birthday!

Knock, knock.
Who's there?
Chimp.
Chimp who?
Chimp off the old block.

Knock, knock.
Who's there?
Fiona.
Fiona who?
Fiona lookout for Mom and Dad.

Knock, knock.
Who's there?
Nana.
Nana who?
Nana your business!

Knock, knock.
Who's there?
Stepfather.
Stepfather who?
One stepfather and you'll be inside.

Knock, knock.
Who's there?
Eliza.
Eliza who?
Eliza wake at night thinking about monsters
under his bed.

Knock, knock.
Who's there?
Jessie.
Jessie who?
Jessie that man over there? That's my dad.

Knock, knock.
Who's there?
Who's.
Who's who?
You're the dad and I'm the son!

Knock, knock.
Who's there?
Mustache.
Mustache who?
I mustache you a question, so let me in!

Knock, knock.
Who's there?
Ashley.
Ashley who?
Ashley I changed my mind and I don't want to come in.

Knock, knock.
Who's there?
Justice.
Justice who?
Justice I thought—no one home.

Knock, knock.
Who's there?
Darlene.
Darlene who?
Please be a Darlene and open the door for me.

Knock, knock.
Who's there?
Sincerely.
Sincerely who?
Sincerely this morning, I've been waiting for you to open this door.

Knock, knock.
Who's there?
Sloane.
Sloane who?
Sloane-ly outside. Please let me in!

Knock, knock.
Who's there?
Adore.
Adore who?
Adore stands between us. Open up!

Knock, knock.
Who's there?
Stopwatch.
Stopwatch who?
Stopwatch you're doing and open the door.

Knock, knock.
Who's there?
Usher.
Usher who?
Usher wish you would let me in.

Knock, knock.
Who's there?
Winner.
Winner who?
Winner you going to let me in?

Knock, knock.
Who's there?
Wire.
Wire who?
Wire you not opening the door?

Knock, knock.
Who's there?
Andy.
Andy who?
Andy knocked, Andy knocked, but you won't let him in!

Knock, knock.
Who's there?
Dale.
Dale who?
Dale be big trouble if you don't open the door.

Knock, knock.

Who's there?

A little boy.

A little boy who?

A little boy who can't reach the doorbell.

Knock, knock.

Who's there?

Otto.

Otto who?

Otto my way, I'm coming in!

Knock, knock.

Who's there?

Annie.

Annie who?

Annie one home?

Knock, knock.

Who's there?

Simon.

Simon who?

Simon the other side of the door. If you opened up, you'd see!

Knock, knock.

Who's there?

Udder.

Udder who?

Udder people let me in. Why won't you?

Knock, knock.
Who's there?
Acid.
Acid who?
Acid I would stop by, so here I am!

Knock, knock.
Who's there?
Bailey.
Bailey who?
I know you Bailey know me, but can I come in?

Knock, knock.
Who's there?
Avery.
Avery who?
Avery nice person is knocking on the door.
You should come take a look.

Knock, knock.
Who's there?
Isadore.
Isadore who?
Isadore bell here? I'm tired of knocking.

Knock, knock.
Who's there?
Eva.
Eva who?
Eva you're hard of hearing, or your doorbell isn't working.

Knock, knock.
Who's there?
Garden.
Garden who?
Stop garden the door and let me in!

Knock, knock.
Who's there?
Anna.
Anna who?
Anna chance you'll let me in? It's cold out here!

Knock, knock.
Who's there?
Dozen.
Dozen who?
Dozen anyone want to let me in?

Knock, knock.

Who's there?

Emma.

Emma who?

Emma bit cold out here—
please let me in.

Knock, knock.

Who's there?

Adam.

Adam who?

Adam my way, please. I'm coming in!

Knock, knock.

Who's there?

Disarm.

Disarm who?

Disarm hurts from all the knocking.

Knock, knock.

Who's there?

Dish.

Dish who?

Dish must be a world record
for knocking!

Knock, knock.
Who's there?
Abbot.
Abbot who?
Abbot time you asked!

Knock, knock.
Who's there?
Argue.
Argue who?
Argue going to let me in or not?

Knock, knock.
Who's there?
Aldon.
Aldon who?
When you're Aldon with dinner can you come out and play?

Knock, knock.
Who's there?
Juan.
Juan who?
Juan of these days, you'll open the door.

Knock, knock.
Who's there?
June.
June who?
June know how long I've been knocking out here?

Knock, knock.
Who's there?
Fozzie.
Fozzie who?
Fozzie hundredth time, let me in!

Knock, knock.
Who's there?
Olive.
Olive who?
Olive here, so you'd better let me in.

Knock, knock.
Who's there?
Archie.
Archie who?
Archie going to let me in?

Knock, knock.
Who's there?
Alex.
Alex who?
Alex-plain later—just let me in.

Knock, knock.
Who's there?
Isaiah.
Isaiah who?
Isaiah nothing until you open this door!

Knock, knock.
Who's there?
Alibi.
Alibi who?
Alibi you a box of candy if you open the door.

Knock, knock.
Who's there?
Doris.
Doris who?
Doris locked. That's why
I'm knocking.

Knock, knock.
Who's there?
Bean.
Bean who?
Bean here for ages.
What's kept you?

Knock, knock.

Who's there?

Heywood, Hugh, and Harry.

Heywood, Hugh, and Harry who?

Heywood Hugh Harry up and open the door?

Knock, knock.

Who's there?

Maple.

Maple who?

I maple the door off its hinges if you don't open it.

Knock, knock.
Who's there?
Anatole.
Anatole who?
Anatole me you'd be coming over today.

Knock, knock.
Who's there?
Allison.
Allison who?
Allison for someone to come to the door
but I don't hear anyone coming.

Knock, knock.
Who's there?
Luke.
Luke who?
Luke through the keyhole and you'll see.

Knock, knock.
Who's there?
Gino.
Gino who?
Gino me—now open the door!

Knock, knock.
Who's there?
Arlo.
Arlo who?
Arlo temperature is making me cold. Please let me in!

Knock, knock.
Who's there?
Orange.
Orange who?
Orange you going to let me in?

Knock, knock.
Who's there?
Oliver.
Oliver who?
Oliver doors are locked. Let me in!

Knock, knock.
Who's there?
Frank.
Frank who?
Can I be Frank and say I really want you to open the door?

Knock, knock.

Who's there?
Defeat.
Defeat who?
Defeat are
hurting. Can I come
in and sit down?

Knock, knock.
Who's there?
Dishes.
Dishes who?
Dishes me. Can I come in?

Knock, knock.
Who's there?
Elba.
Elba who?
Elba happy to see you when you
open the door.

Knock, knock.
Who's there?
Ethan.
Ethan who?
Ethan if you don't open the door, I'll still like you.

Knock, knock.
Who's there?
Ear.
Ear who?
Ear you are. I've been looking everywhere.

Knock, knock.
Who's there?
Sara.
Sara who?
Sara doorbell around here?

Knock, knock.
Who's there?
Ferdie.
Ferdie who?
Ferdie last time, open up!

Knock, knock.
Who's there?
Ivan.
Ivan who?
Ivan to come in, so please open the door!

Knock, knock.
Who's there?
Jonah.
Jonah who?
Jonah anybody who will open the door for me?

Knock, knock.
Who's there?
Miniature.
Miniature who?
The miniature open the door I'll tell you.

Knock, knock.
Who's there?
Lee.
Lee who?
I'm lone Lee without you. Please let me in!

Knock, knock.
Who's there?
Eyes.
Eyes who?
Eyes better come in before I catch a cold.

Knock, knock.
Who's there?
Hair.
Hair who?
Hair you are!

Knock, knock.
Who's there?
Ida.
Ida who?
Ida know, I gotta ask.

Knock, knock.
Who's there?
Iva.
Iva who?
Iva sore hand from
knocking so much!

Knock, knock.

Who's there?

Isaac.

Isaac who?

Isaac of knocking, so please let me in!

Knock, knock.

Who's there?

Misty.

Misty who?

I Misty chance to see you—will you let me come in?

Laugh Around The World

Knock, knock.
Who's there?
Arctics.
Arctics who?
Arctics going to bite me in the woods?

Knock, knock.
Who's there?
Alaska.
Alaska who?
Alaska my mom if I can come out and play.

Knock, knock.
Who's there?
Congo.
Congo who?
Congo out—I'm grounded.

Knock, knock.
Who's there?
Iowa.
Iowa who?
Iowa you a dollar.

Knock, knock.
Who's there?
Kansas.
Kansas who?
Kansas what soda comes in.

Knock, knock.
Who's there?
Dublin.
Dublin who?
The cost of milk is Dublin.

Knock, knock.
Who's there?
Cairo.
Cairo who?
Cairo the boat now?

Knock, knock.
Who's there?
Samoa.
Samoa who?
Samoa cake, please!

Knock, knock.
Who's there?
Sicily.
Sicily who?
Sicily question.

Knock, knock.
Who's there?
Kenya.
Kenya who?
Kenya guess who it is?

Knock, knock.
Who's there?
Asia.
Asia who?
Asia mother home from work yet?

Knock, knock.
Who's there?
Cuba.
Cuba who?
Cuba ice.

Knock, knock.

Who's there?

Minneapolis.

Minneapolis who?

Minneapolis a day keeps many doctors away.

Knock, knock.

Who's there?

Erie.

Erie who?

Erie comes and he looks angry!

Knock, knock.

Who's there?

Marilyn.

Marilyn who?

Marilyn is a state just
north of Virginia.

Knock, knock.

Who's there?

Madrid.

Madrid who?

Madrid you wash my jeans?

Knock, knock.

Who's there?

Annapolis.

Annapolis who?

Annapolis a tasty fruit.

Knock, knock.
Who's there?
Paris.
Paris who?
Paris my favorite fruit.

Knock, knock.
Who's there?
Taiwan.
Taiwan who?
Taiwan shoe and leave the other untied.

Knock, knock.
Who's there?
Albany.
Albany who?
Albany-ing help with my homework!

Knock, knock.
Who's there?
Hawaii.
Hawaii who?
Fine, Hawaii you?

Knock, knock.

Who's there?

Yukon.

Yukon who?

Yukon lead a horse to water,
but you can't make it drink.

Knock, knock.
Who's there?
Israel.
Israel who?
Israel good to be here.

Knock, knock.
Who's there?
Francis.
Francis who?
Francis in Europe.

Knock, knock.
Who's there?
Everest.
Everest who?
Everest from telling knock-knock jokes?

Knock, knock.

Who's there?

Italy.

Italy who?

Italy a shame if you don't open this door!

Knock, knock.

Who's there?

Fresno.

Fresno who?

Fresno fun when he's grouchy.

Knock, knock.
Who's there?
Europe.
Europe who?
Europe to no good, aren't you?

Knock, knock.

Who's there?

Arkansas.

Arkansas who?

Arkansas through any piece of
wood in less than five seconds!

Knock, knock.
Who's there?
Arizona.
Arizona who?
Arizona room for one of us in this town.

Knock, knock.
Who's there?
Ghana.
Ghana who?
We're Ghana go to the movies.

Knock, knock.
Who's there?
Florida.
Florida who?
The Florida bathroom is wet.

Knock, knock.
Who's there?
Genoa.
Genoa who?
Genoa any new jokes?

Knock, knock.
Who's there?
Dakota.
Dakota who?
Dakota is too short in the arms for me.

Knock, knock.

Who's there?

Japan.

Japan who?

Ouch, Japan is too hot.

Knock, knock.

Who's there?

Spain.

Spain who?

Spain to have to keep knocking on this door!

Knock, knock.

Who's there?

Tijuana.

Tijuana who?

Tijuana play some one-on-one?

Knock, knock.
Who's there?
Oslo.
Oslo who?
Oslo down—there's no hurry.

Knock, knock.
Who's there?
Burma.
Burma who?
Burma hand on the stove.

Knock, knock.
Who's there?
Rio.
Rio who?
Rio funny, wise-guy. You know it's me.

Knock, knock.
Who's there?
Zippy.
Zippy who?
Mrs. Zippy.

Knock, knock.
Who's there?
Costas.
Costas who?
Costas a fortune to get to Australia.

Knock, knock.
Who's there?
Babylon.
Babylon who?
Babylon. I'm not really listening.

Knock, knock.
Who's there?
Venice.
Venice who?
Venice this door going to open?

Knock, knock.
Who's there?
Yukon.
Yukon who?
Yukon say that again.

Knock, knock.
Who's there?
Wyoming.
Wyoming who?
Wyoming so mean to me?

Knock, knock.
Who's there?
Quebec.
Quebec who?
Quebec to the end of the line.

Knock, knock.
Who's there?
Aspen.
Aspen who?
Aspen thinking about you all day.

Knock, knock.
Who's there?
Bayou.
Bayou who?
I'll bayou a treat.

Knock, knock.
Who's there?
Indonesia.
Indonesia who?
Spiders make me weak
Indonesia.

Knock, knock.
Who's there?
Armenia.
Armenia who?
Armenia every word I say.

Knock, knock.
Who's there?
Irving.
Irving who?
Irving a wonderful time; wish you were here!

Knock, knock.
Who's there?
Iran.
Iran who?
Iran hard to get here.

Knock, knock.
Who's there?
Juneau.
Juneau who?
Juneau the capital of Alaska?

Knock, knock.
Who's there?
Tennessee.
Tennessee who?
Tennessee you later?

Knock, knock.
Who's there?
Texas.
Texas who?
Texas are getting higher every year.

Knock, knock.
Who's there?
Germany.
Germany who?
Germany people are knocking at your door?

Knock, knock.
Who's there?
Never Never Land.
Never Never Land who?
Never Never Land money to
a stranger.

Knock, knock.
Who's there?
Bolivia.
Bolivia who?
Bolivia me—I know what I'm talking about.

Knock, knock.
Who's there?
Heavy.
Heavy who?
Heavy ever been to Japan?

Knock, knock.
Who's there?
Havana.
Havana who?
We're Havana great time.

Knock, knock.
Who's there?
India.
India who?
India nighttime I go to sleep.

Knock, knock.
Who's there?
Pencil.
Pencil who?
Pencil-vania's bigger
than Delaware.

Knock, knock.
Who's there?
Odessa.
Odessa who?
Odessa good one!

Knock, knock.
Who's there?
Tibet.
Tibet who?
Early Tibet and early to rise.

Knock, knock.
Who's there?
Perth.
Perth who?
A Perth full of cointh.

Knock, knock.
Who's there?
Nantucket.
Nantucket who?
Nantucket, but she'll give it back.

Knock, knock.
Who's there?
Idaho.
Idaho who?
If Idaho, Idaho the
whole garden.

Knock, knock.
Who's there?
Missouri.
Missouri who?
Missouri loves company.

Knock, knock.
Who's there?
Moscow.
Moscow who?
I Moscow home soon.

Knock, knock.
Who's there?
Norway.
Norway who?
Norway will I leave till you open this door.

Knock, knock.
Who's there?
Italian.
Italian who?
Italian you for the last time—open this door!

Knock, knock.
Who's there?
Uruguay.
Uruguay who?
You go Uruguay and I'll go mine.

Knock, knock.
Who's there?
Uganda.
Uganda who?
Uganda get away with this!

Knock, knock.

Who's there?

Kentucky.

Kentucky who?

Dad Kentucky you in at night.

Knock, knock.

Who's there?

Utah.

Utah who?

Utah-ing to me? I can't hear you.

Knock, knock.

Who's there?

Sahara.

Sahara who?

Sahara you feeling today?

Wacky Weather

Knock, knock.
Who's there?
Lorraine.
Lorraine who?
Lorraine is falling. Where's my umbrella?

Knock, knock.
Who's there?
Scold.
Scold who?
Scold outside.

Knock, knock.
Who's there?
Frostbite.
Frostbite who?
Frostbite your food, then chew it.

Knock, knock.
Who's there?
August.
August who?
August of wind almost blew me away!

Knock, knock.
Who's there?
Gladys.
Gladys who?
Gladys summer, aren't you?

Knock, knock.
Who's there?
Stephanie.
Stephanie who?
It's Stephanie going to be sunny today.

Knock, knock.
Who's there?
Morrison.
Morrison who?
The Morrison, the more I tan.

Knock, knock.
Who's there?
Sleet.
Sleet who?
Sleet—I'm starving.

Knock, knock.
Who's there?
Hansel.
Hansel who?
Hansel freeze if you
don't wear gloves.

Knock, knock.
Who's there?
Bennett.
Bennett who?
Bennett rains it pours.

Knock, knock.
Who's there?
Freeze.
Freeze who?
"Freeze a jolly good fellow, freeze a jolly
good fellow . . ."

Knock, knock.
Who's there?
Snow.
Snow who?
Snow one's better than you.

Knock, knock.
Who's there?
Wet.
Wet who?
Wet me in—it's waining!

Knock, knock.
Who's there?
Icy.
Icy who?
Icy you opening the door!

Knock, knock.
Who's there?
Macon.
Macon who?
Macon the best of standing here in the cold.

Knock, knock.
Who's there?
Hot air.
Hot air who?
Hot air, pardner, how ya doin'?

Knock, knock.
Who's there?
Butter.
Butter who?
Butter bring an umbrella—it looks like rain.

Knock, knock.
Who's there?
Stanton.
Stanton who?
Stanton here in the cold is no fun.

Knock, knock.
Who's there?
Snowy.
Snowy who?
Snowy in the word snow—
it's spelled s-n-o-w.

Knock, knock.
Who's there?
Dancer.
Dancer is simple; it wasn't a ghost—
it was only the wind!

This and That

Knock, knock.

Who's there?

Adair.

Adair who?

Adair once but now I'm bald.

Knock, knock.
Who's there?
Haven.
Haven who?
Haven you heard enough of these knock-knock jokes?

Knock, knock.
Who's there?
I am.
I am who?
You mean you don't remember who you are?

Knock, knock.
Who's there?
Ooze.
Ooze who?
Ooze in charge here?

Knock, knock.
Who's there?
Baron.
Baron who?
Baron mind who you're talking to.

Knock, knock.
Who's there?
Boil.
Boil who?
Boil you like this next joke!

Knock, knock.
Who's there?
Just oodle.
Just oodle who?
Just oodle you think you're talking to?

Knock, knock.
Who's there?
Says.
Says who?
Says me, that's who.

Knock, knock.
Who's there?
Saturn.
Saturn who?
Saturn my phone and now it won't work.

Knock, knock.
Who's there?
Alda.
Alda who?
Alda kids like my knock-knock jokes.

Knock, knock.
Who's there?
Safari.
Safari who?
Safari so good!

Knock, knock.
Who's there?
Beth.
Beth who?
Beth time ever.

Knock, knock.
Who's there?
Switch.
Switch who?
Switch lollipop would you like?

Knock, knock.
Who's there?
Amnesia.
Amnesia who?
I don't remember.

Knock, knock.
Who's there?
Foster.
Foster who?
Foster than a speeding bullet!

Knock, knock.
Who's there?
Gable.
Gable who?
Gable to leap tall buildings in a
single bound.

Knock, knock.
Who's there?
Voodoo.
Voodoo who?
Voodoo you think you are?

Knock, knock.
Who's there?
Countess.
Countess who?
Does this countess a funny knock-knock joke?

Knock, knock.
Who's there?
Hacienda.
Hacienda who?
Hacienda the joke!

Knock, knock.
Who's there?
Cain.
Cain who?
Cain you tell me a knock-knock joke?

Knock, knock.
Who's there?
Disguise.
Disguise who?
Disguise de limit.

Knock, knock.
Who's there?
Noise.
Noise who?
Noise to see you! How have you been?

Knock, knock.
Who's there?
Tummy.
Tummy who?
Tummy you'll always be number one.

Knock, knock.
Who's there?
Amora.
Amora who?
Amora I see, Amora I like.

Knock, knock.
Who's there?
Quill.
Quill who?
Quill we meet again?

Knock, knock.
Who's there?
Blush.
Blush who?
Thanks, but I didn't sneeze.

Knock, knock.
Who's there?
Scald.
Scald who?
Scald working together, my friend—
that's teamwork.

Knock, knock.
Who's there?
Commit.
Commit who?
Commit me and we'll go places.

Knock, knock.
Who's there?
Army.
Army who?
Army and you still friends?

Knock, knock.
Who's there?
Mission.
Mission who?
Mission you lots—wish you were here!

Knock, knock.
Who's there?
Myth.
Myth who?
Myth you, too.

Knock, knock.
Who's there?
Interrupting pirate.
Interrupting pir—
ARRRRRRR!

Knock, knock.
Who's there?
Isle.
Isle who?
Isle ask the questions around here.

Knock, knock.
Who's there?
Amy.
Amy who?
Amy in the right direction.

Knock, knock.
Who's there?
Cozy.
Cozy who?
Cozy who's knocking.

Knock, knock.
Who's there?
Summer.
Summer who?
Summer these jokes are funny, but some aren't!

Knock, knock.
Who's there?
Hatch.
Hatch who?
Ha ha, made you sneeze!

Knock, knock.

Who's there?

Unite.

Unite who?

When unite Lancelot, he joins
the Round Table.

Knock, knock.

Who's there?

Ahmed.

Ahmed who?

Ahmed a big mistake coming here.

Knock, knock.

Who's there?

Uno.

Uno who?

Uno who this is!

Knock, knock.
Who's there?
Throat.
Throat who?
Throat out if it's spoiled.

Knock, knock.
Who's there?
Easily distractible.
Easily distractible who?
I'm sorry, were you talking to me?

Knock, knock.
Who's there?
Alex.
Alex who?
Alex the questions around here!

Knock, knock.
Who's there?
Boo.
Boo who?
Don't cry! It's just a joke.

Knock, knock.
Who's there?
Eyesore.
Eyesore who?
Eyesore do like you.

Knock, knock.
Who's there?
Armani.
Armani who?
Armani is all spent, so now we need to earn more.

Knock, knock.
Who's there?
Saddle.
Saddle who?
Saddle be the day.

Knock, knock.
Who's there?
Hoover.
Hoover who?
Hoover you expecting?

Knock, knock.

Who's there?

Scurry.

Scurry who?

Scurry monsters live in the swamp!

Knock, knock.

Who's there?

Heaven.

Heaven who?

Heaven seen you in ages.

Knock, knock.

Who's there?

July.

July who?

July awake at night counting sheep?

Knock, knock.
Who's there?
Thumb.
Thumb who?
Thumb like it hot and thumb like it cold.

Knock, knock.
Who's there?
Ears.
Ears who?
Ears looking at you, kid.

Knock, knock.
Who's there?
Torch.
Torch who?
Torch you'd never ask.

Knock, knock.
Who's there?
Tank.
Tank who?
You're welcome.

Knock, knock
Who's there?
Uphill.
Uphill who?
Uphill will help your headache go away.

Knock, knock.
Who's there?
Comma.
Comma who?
Comma little closer and I'll tell you.

Knock, knock.
Who's there?
Zookeeper.
Zookeeper who?
Zookeeper away from me. She's mean!

Knock, knock.
Who's there?
Ghost.
Ghost who?
Ghost to show you don't
remember my name!

Knock, knock.
Who's there?
Heart.
Heart who?
Heart to hear you—speak up.

Knock, knock.
Who's there?
Bashful.
Bashful who?
Sorry, I can't tell you. I'm too embarrassed.

Knock, knock.
Who's there?
Nobel.
Nobel who?
There was Nobel, so I had to knock!

Knock, knock.
Who's there?
Major.
Major who?
Major open the door, didn't I?

Knock, knock.
Who's there?
Hair.
Hair who?
Hair today, gone tomorrow.

Knock, knock.
Who's there?
Senior.
Senior who?
Senior being so nosy, I'm not going to tell you.

Knock, knock.
Who's there?
Statue.
Statue who?
Statue making all
that noise?

Knock, knock.
Who's there?
Dummy.
Dummy who?
Will you dummy a favor, please?

Knock, knock.
Who's there?
Yachts.
Yachts who?
Yachts up, doc?

Knock, knock.
Who's there?
Butcher.
Butcher who?
Butcher hand over your heart when you say the Pledge of Allegiance.

Knock, knock.
Who's there?
Beta.
Beta who?
Beta be good or you'll be in trouble.

Knock, knock.
Who's there?
Waddle.
Waddle who?
Waddle you give me if I go away?

Knock, knock.
Who's there?
Quarter.
Quarter who?
Quarter with her hand in the cookie jar!

Knock, knock.
Who's there?
Russian.
Russian who?
Russian about will wear you out.

Knock, knock.
Who's there?
Cash.
Cash who?
Cash me if you can.

Knock, knock.
Who's there?
Wood.
Wood who?
Wood you laugh at my jokes?

Knock, knock.
Who's there?
Bond.
Bond who?
You're Bond to succeed if you work hard.

Knock, knock.
Who's there?
Aspen.
Aspen who?
When Aspen around I get dizzy.

Knock, knock.
Who's there?
Ears.
Ears who?
Ears another knock-knock joke!

Knock, knock.
Who's there?
Eyes.
Eyes who?
Eyes have one more knock-knock joke!

Knock, knock.
Who's there?
Chin.
Chin who?
Chin up! That was the last joke.

Knock, knock.

Who's there?

Cargo.

Cargo who?

No, cargo beep, beep.

Knock, knock.
Who's there?
Icon.
Icon who?
Icon tell you another knock-knock joke if you want!

Knock, knock.
Who's there?
Topic.
Topic who?
Topic a wildflower is against the law.

Knork, knork.
Who's there?
Shirley.
Shirley who?
Shirley there must be something wrong with your door knocker.

Knock, knock.
Who's there?
Byte.
Byte who?
Byte you're happy to see me again.

Will you remember me in an hour?
Yes.
Will you remember me in a day?
Yes.
Will you remember me in a week?
Yes.
I think you won't.
Yes, I will.
Knock knock.
Who's there?
See? You've forgotten me already!

Knock, knock.
Who's there?
Habit.
Habit who?
Habit your way, I'll come back later.

Knock, knock.
Who's there?
Tex.
Tex who?
It Tex two to tango.

Knock, knock.
Who's there?
Z.
Z who?
Z you in the morning!

Knock, knock.
Who's there?
Hugh Juan.
Hugh Juan who?
Hugh Juan a prize. Open
the door.

Knock, knock.
Who's there?
Hygiene.
Hygiene who?
Hygiene! What's new with you, Gene?

Knock, knock.
Who's there?
Nickel.
Nickel who?
Nickel vouch for me. Just ask Nick.

Knock, knock.
Who's there?
Ash.
Ash who?
It sounds like you're catching a cold.

Knock, knock.
Who's there?
Atomic.
Atomic who?
Atomic-ache is no fun at all!

Knock, knock.
Who's there?
Dare.
Dare who?
Dare, dare. It's OK!

Knock, knock.

Who's there?

Nose.

Nose who?

Nose any more knock-knock jokes?

Knock, knock.
Who's there?
Wheel.
Wheel who?
Wheel stop coming over if we're not invited.

Knock, knock.
Who's there?
Oil change.
Oil change who?
Oil change. Just give me another chance.

Knock, knock.
Who's there?
Colin.
Colin who?
Colin all cars!

Knock, knock.
Who's there?
Vaughn.
Vaughn who?
Vaughn day my
prince will come.

Knock, knock.
Who's there?
Baldwin.
Baldwin who?
You might be Baldwin you're older.

Knock, knock.
Who's there?
Adair.
Adair who?
Adair to be different.

Knock, knock.
Who's there?
Hobbit.
Hobbit who?
Sorry, telling knock-knock jokes is a bad hobbit I'm trying
to break.

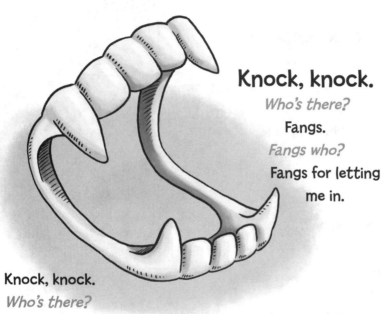

Knock, knock.
Who's there?
Fangs.
Fangs who?
Fangs for letting
me in.

Knock, knock.
Who's there?
Hideout.
Hideout who?
Hideout you even thought it was possible.

Knock, knock.
Who's there?
Bargain.
Bargain who?
Bargain up the wrong tree.

Knock, knock.
Who's there?
Tree.
Tree who?
Tree more days till vacation.

Knock, knock.
Who's there?
Wafer.
Wafer who?
Wafer me—I'm coming, too!

Knock, knock.
Who's there?
Spin.
Spin who?
Spin too long since we saw each other.

Knock, knock.
Who's there?
Mecca.
Mecca who?
You Mecca me happy.

Knock, knock.

Who's there?

Yacht.

Yacht who?

Yacht to know me by now!

Knock, knock.

Who's there?

Cotton.

Cotton who?

Cotton a trap—please get me out!

Knock, knock.

Who's there?

Verdi.

Verdi who?

Verdi been all day?

Knock, knock.
Who's there?
Column.
Column who?
Column down. Things will be all right.

Knock, knock.
Who's there?
Welcome.
Welcome who?
Welcome up to see you again soon!

Knock, knock.
Who's there?
Meter.
Meter who?
Let's meter at the park.

Knock, knock.
Who's there?
Scott.
Scott who?
There's Scott to be a better knock-knock joke
than this one!

Knock, knock.
Who's there?
Sizzle.
Sizzle who?
Sizzle need your full attention.

Knock, knock.
Who's there?
Vampire.
Vampire who?
The Vampire State
Building.

Knock, knock.
Who's there?
Summertime.
Summertime who?
Summertime you can be a real pest.

Knock, knock.
Who's there?
Fannie.
Fannie who?
Fannie body asks, I'm not home.

Knock, knock.
Who's there?
Huron.
Huron who?
Huron on my toe, could you please step off it?

Knock, knock.
Who's there?
Ya.
Ya who?
Giddyup, cowboy!

Knock, knock.
Who's there?
Boomerang.
Boomerang who?
Boomerang the doorbell. Guess we should let him in!

Knock, knock.
Who's there?
Sombrero.
Sombrero who?
Sombrero-ver the rainbow.

Knock, knock.
Who's there?
Gargoyle.
Gargoyle who?
If you gargoyle with salt
water, your throat will
feel better.

Knock, knock.
Who's there?
Avenue.
Avenue who?
Avenue heard enough of these jokes?

Knock, knock.
Who's there?
Yellow.
Yellow who?
Yellow, and how are you doing today?

Knock, knock.
Who's there?
B.C.
B.C. who?
B.C.-ing you soon.

Knock, knock.
Who's there?
Weed.
Weed who?
Weed better go home—it's time for lunch.

Knock, knock.
Who's there?
Sparkle.
Sparkle who?
Sparkle start a fire if you're not careful.

Knock, knock.
Who's there?
Peeka.
Peeka who?
Peeka-boo!

Knock, knock.

Who's there?

Police.

Police who?

Police stop telling knock-knock jokes.

Knock, knock.
Who's there?
Crypt.
Crypt who?
She crypt up behind me.

Knock, knock.
Who's there?
Disaster.
Disaster who?
Disaster be my lucky day.

Knock, knock.
Who's there?
Dots.
Dots who?
Dots not important.

Knock, knock.
Who's there?
Soldier.
Soldier who?
Soldier house yet?

Knock, knock.
Who's there?
Dunce.
Dunce who?
Dunce say another word.

Knock, knock.
Who's there?
Element.
Element who?
Element to tell you that she can't see you today.

Knock, knock.
Who's there?
Zoom.
Zoom who?
Zoom did you expect?

Knock, knock.
Who's there?
Toothy.
Toothy who?
Toothy is the day after
Monday.

Knock, knock.
Who's there?
Hi.
Hi who?
"Hi ho! Hi ho! It's off to work we go."

Knock, knock.
Who's there?
Repeat.
Repeat who?
Who, who, who . . .

Knock, knock.
Who's there?
Queen.
Queen who?
Queen as a whistle.

Knock, knock.
Who's there?
Waiter.
Waiter who?
Waiter minute while I tie my shoes.

Knock, knock.
Who's there?
Zany.
Zany who?
Zanybody have some carrots? I'm hungry!

Knock, knock.
Who's there?
Wah.
Wah who?
Well, you don't have to get so excited about it.

Knock, knock.

Who's there?

Island.

Island who?

Island in your backyard
with my parachute.

Knock, knock.

Who's there?

Tide.

Tide who?

Are you tide of knock-knock jokes yet?

Knock, knock.

Who's there?

Lass.

Lass who?

That's what cowboys use to rope calves, isn't it?

Knock, knock.

Who's there?

You.

You who?

Did you call me?

Knock, knock.
Who's there?
Nuisance.
Nuisance who?
What's nuisance yesterday?

Knock, knock.
Who's there?
Ogre.
Ogre who?
Please do it ogre again.

Knock, knock.
Who's there?
Weaver.
Weaver who?
Weaver alone, you
mean monster!

Knock, knock.
Who's there?
Wedge.
Wedge who?
Wedge you get those sunglasses?

Knock, knock.
Who's there?
Tail.
Tail who?
Tail everyone you know.

Knock, knock.
Who's there?
Passion.
Passion who?
Passion through and thought I'd say hello.

Knock, knock.
Who's there?
Qualify.
Qualify who?
I'll qualify ever want to tell you.

Knock, knock.
Who's there?
Wendy.
Wendy who?
Wendy you think we'll be done with
these knock-knock jokes?

Knock, knock.
Who's there?
Zone.
Zone who?
He's scared of his zone shadow.

Knock, knock.
Who's there?
Oldest.
Oldest who?
Oldest knocking is giving me a headache.

Knock, knock.
Who's there?
Quilty.
Quilty who?
Quilty as charged.

Knock, knock.
Who's there?
Zoo.
Zoo who?
Zoo think you can
come out and play?

Knock, knock.
Who's there?
Weirdo.
Weirdo who?
Weirdo you think you're going?

Knock, knock.
Who's there?
Witches.
Witches who?
Witches the way to go home?

Knock, knock.
Who's there?
Wooden shoe.
Wooden shoe who?
Wooden shoe like to know!

Knock, knock.
Who's there?
Tootle.
Tootle who?
Goodbye to you, too.

Knock, knock.
Who's there?
Thistle.
Thistle who?
Thistle be the last joke in this book.